Pursuing The Mystery Of Perfection

Growing In Grace and Knowledge

By *Jelani Faraja Kafela*

Dec 11, 2011

Pursuing The Mystery of Perfection

Growing In Grace and Knowledge

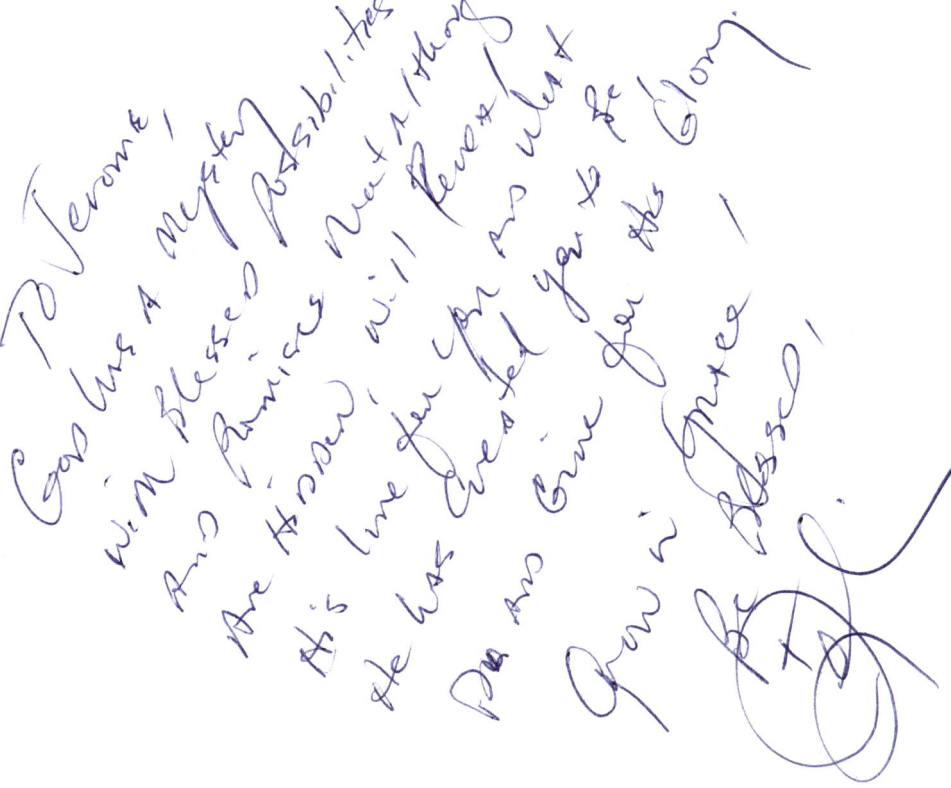

© Copyright 2010 Jelani Faraja Kafela

All rights reserved. This book is protected under the copyright laws of the United States of America. No portion of this book may be reproduced in any form, without the written permission of the publisher. Permission granted on request.

Unlock Publishing House
231 West Hampton Place
Capitol Heights, MD 20743
www.unlockpublishinghouse.com
1 (240) 619-3852

Cover Design and Artwork: Jason Muldrow
Page Layout and Editing: Rosita Dozier

Unlock Publishing House is not responsible for any content or determination of work. All information is solely considered as the point of view of the author

ISBN: 978-0982931820

Contents

Acknowledgements ix

Preface xiii

Beautiful Request xxv

PURSUING THE MYSTERY OF PERFECTION

One: God's Mysterious Plan 29

Two: Passionately Pursing the Mystery 103

Three: The Heaven and Earth Project 135

Four: The Incarnational Embrace 141

Five: The Tarnished Cross 151

Six: Living in the Mystery of the Tabernacle 159

GROWING IN GRACE AND IN KNOWLEDGE

You Never Leave 196

Seven: Grow in Grace and In Knowledge 197

Pursuing the Mystery of Ministry 213

Acknowledgements

Truly it is no mystery that serving the Body of Christ takes a shared ministry concept in order to be done sincerely. To love Christ is to serve Christ; to serve Christ is to love Christ. One assumes the other. One cannot love Christ sincerely without serving Christ completely; one cannot serve Christ completely without loving Christ with a pure heart, a good conscience and a sincere faith (I Timothy 1:5).

When the Lord Jesus asked Simon Peter three times following his tragic denials, "Do you love me?" and the apostle answered in the affirmative to each question, Jesus called Peter to a lifetime of service: "Feed my lambs . . . Tend my sheep . . . Feed my sheep Christ said."

Those who love Christ the most, serve Christ the best. When talking to God about this matter of love and Christian service I must confess to God that I do not possess gifts like the apostle Paul, don't always experience the right heart like David, or the strength of conviction like the prophet Jeremiah, nor a host of others within the Christian faith, but like Paul, I must confess that there is something we all can do and that is you and I can love the same Lord Jesus with our all—just as they did.

One of the tragedies of the modern church and what distinguishes the sincerely empowered and empowering church from the self indulgent or superficial one is that we have so many who are trying to serve Christ but who don't have a pure love for Christ and a passionate pursuit of an understanding of the mystery of His perfection. Their service is self-centered service with an admixture—call it contaminated service. They are not serving

Christ with sincere motives but under false pretenses. They only serve Christ for selfish reasons, for what they can get and not what they can do to serve His perfect will.

With this in mind I wish to thank all those who make up the sincere church I am blessed to serve and pastor, who continue to serve Christ with a pure heart, a good conscience and sincere faith as part of the Body of Christ called Imani Temple Christian Fellowship located in Pomona California, in what is called California's Inland Empire.

At Imani, we use a Sincere Church Ministry Model to guide the church as we pursue the mystery of perfection. The Sincere Church Model has as its concept five S's to identify it. *Surrender, Share, Shape, Synergize and Serve.* Using this model I wish to thank the following people.

First, to Lady Kathy, *I sincerely love you* always as my wife, partner and my inspiration; thank you for putting up with me doing this writing thing yet again. I can always find my way on the steady road called you and your encouragement. I wish to thank Jason Muldrow for the cover design and for *creatively sharing the Vision.* You helped to guide and inspire this effort to completion. To Zaina Goggins, thank you daughter for your beautiful poems, and *Connecting the Steps to the Next Generation* needed to pursue the mystery generationally. Your poems are like climbing spiritual ladders to successfully look into our future and seeing that it already shines with faithful young believers like you. Thank you so much for sharing them with us. To Danielle Osonduagwuike, Administrative Adjutant for our Kingdom Council of Elders, thank you for all that you do to help me *Shape the Vision.* Your meditations will help to ground all who will allow them to sow seeds of thought and provide prayers of gratefulness as they seek a deeper relationship with Christ. It is so awesome to know that someone like you loves me and the things God has blessed us to do together. To Rosita Dozier, again, I thank you for your *Guidance and Support of the Vision of this book* as I struggle along this journey to discover the mystery of perfection as an author and visionary. Special thanks to Elder Jeanetta Mitchell for believing in me and this work and we praise God for you as we proudly witness your growth in grace and knowledge of the mystery of your calling. To my publisher, Dawn Harvey, thank you for *Supplying the Vision* of my meanderings through the valley of my own wonderings to discover the wonderful works of God through the publishing of these first two attempts at writing books. I pray that this one blesses you as much as the first.

I want to also thank, Assistant Pastor Sam and Youth Pastor Tamika Casey, for faithfully *Sharing the Spiritual Leadership* as my spiritual son and daughter of this sincere church vision. I dedicate this book to the two of you and to my other spiritual son Elder Akinlana Osonduagwuike for your continued commitment to *Sincerely Shaping the Vision* of the mystery of perfection for all you encounter as a master teacher of the promises of God both in the church and in the community as a Middle School Principal. To Pastor LaTanya Clarke, Deaconess Carlotta Jones and the I-Team, I thank you for providing *Synergy for the Vision* as you serve the people of God as they enter the mystery of perfection called Imani. To Deacon Ronald Robinson and those who share in serving the ministry of the Invisible Hands Food Program, I wish to thank you for *Practically Serving the Vision* of the mystery of perfection as you continue to serve our community faithfully by providing food to those families in need of God's invisible helping hand.

To my brother and sister Hertran Jones and Elder Toni Jones, you, along with Leroy Williams were the first ones I asked to faithfully pursue this mystery of perfection with me and I want to thank you for coming along side of me as partners in *Surrendered Worship to this Vision* twelve years ago. It is no mystery that I will love each of you as my oldest friends always and forever. To Lisa Hudson and the Finance Team thank you for your *Faithful Stewardship of the Vision*. Thank you, to my personal team members Lanita Edwards and Curtis Robinzine for being *Faithful Servants of the Vision* as my armor bearers. To Verna Joseph, the Assistant to the Senior Pastor, along with my cousin Carol Sampson my personal Adjutant word could never express my *sincere gratitude* for all that you do. To Sister Freddie Wright and the Covenant Ushers, thank you for *Standing at the Door Protecting the Vision*. To my cousin Barbara Bishop, as the senior member of our faith family I want to thank you for *Serving my Churchguy Ministries Vision* and for always being there continuing the Spirit of my mother in my life. I miss her but love you for always being there! A special thanks to Elder Rachel Akira Goggins for inspiring the Churchguy Ministries Facebook fan page, your commitment has *synergistically* allowed many to connect to this sincere vision across the country.

To my new *Spiritual Covering* and brothers in Christ, Presiding Bishop Clifton Edwards Jr. and Bishop William Walker and the entire Apex Fellowship of Churches family, thank you for elevating me through my recent election to enter the episcopacy and joining you in *Serving the Cause of Christ* as a bishop in the Lord's church.

To my Imani family, and our church leaders, members, and *all who serve with me faithfully* at Imani along with our ministry partners of the Bridge Network you know who you are, thank you for making the work of the ministry so awesome because I get to do it with people like you. There is no greater church within the mystery. Promise me that you will continue to move forward and I promise you that the best is still yet to come as we are perfected in the mystery of it all.

Preface:

" . . . And he gave some apostles; and some, prophets; and some, evangelists;

*and some, pastors and teachers; for the **perfecting** of the saints, for the work of the ministry,*

for the edifying of the body of Christ. " (Ephesians 4:11-12)

Scripture informs us that there are in reality two realms; one is that which is seen, and that which is unseen or remains a mystery. The first is apparent and is the world we know through our minds and five senses. If it were not for divine revelation, we would probably be locked into this level without any way of breaking into the second realm or realizing the importance of pursuing this mystery beyond our senses and the limits of our understanding which is the ultimate reality.

Bound by these limits of time, space, understanding and human control, we would never be able to find true meaning and discover the ultimate purpose for our lives that can only be realized by the mystery of the infinite, absolute and eternal perfectedness of God's person, purpose and plan.

The death of Jesus Christ is a subject of never ending interest to all who study prayerfully the Scripture of Truth. Four words and elements appear to sum up the important features of this Mystery of mysteries: the Death of Christ, (clarity), unnatural (capacity), pre-natural (commitment), and supernatural (consciousness). What does this all mean?

First, the death of Christ was natural, meaning that it was a real death, which requires clarity to understand its implications and possibilities. It is because we are so familiar with the fact of it that the statement appears so simple and much too familiar to us all. But what we find here is one of the wonders of the mystery of God's perfection. The One who was taken by wicked hands "crucified and slain" was none other than Emmanuel – God with us. The blood that was shed on the accursed tree was divine – Thus the church of God was purchased with His own (perfect) blood" (Acts 20:28).

Second, the death of Christ was un-natural. Meaning it was abnormal. But in its perfection we acquired the capacity to live, move and have our being in Christ who died to redeem us. By becoming incarnate, the Son of God became capable of suffering death, yet it must not be inferred from this that death therefore had a claim on Him. This is far from being the case in fact the very opposite was true. Death is the wages of sin, and He has none. Before His birth, it was said to Mary, "that holy thing which shall be born of thee shall be called the Son of God" (Luke 1:35). Not only did Jesus enter the world without contacting the defilement attached to fallen human nature, but He 'did not sin" (I Peter 2:22), "had no sin" (I John 3:5), "knew no sin" (2 Corinthians 5:21). In other words He entered the mystery of life perfect. In person and conduct, He was the Holy One of God without blemish and without spot" (I Peter 1:19). As such, the imperfection of death had no claim on Him. By this He made it capable to believe in Him and have life in our pursuit of the mystery of perfection seen in living His Christ-life.

Third, the Death of Christ was pre–natural. By this the scholars say it was marked out and determined for Him beforehand. He was the Lamb slain from the foundation of the world (Revelation 13:8). Before Adam was created, the Fall was anticipated. Before sin entered the world, salvation from it had been perfectly planned by God. Through the undergirding of the Cross and approaching death, God justly passed over former sins (Romans 3:25). Had not Christ been, in the mystery of God, the Lamb slain from the foundation of the world, every sinning person in the Old Testament times would have gone down to the pit the moment he or she sinned. So would we. In Christ was God's perfect plan for redeeming the world in Christ's commitment to do the will of His Father.

Fourth, the death of Christ was super-natural. By this we mean that it was different from every other death. In all things He has the preeminence. His birth was different, His life was different, and His death was different from all others. He says so Himself when He said, "Therefore does My Father love me, because I lay down my life, that I might take it again. No man takes it from Me, but I lay it down Myself. I have power to . . . take it again" (John 10:17-18). In this we are conscious as we pursue the mystery of His perfect plan.

What we fail to see at all as the sincere church is this was just the work He was called to do! So he finished His work, now seats at the right hand of the Father, in the perfected place, and calls us, those who would move forward through His grace and knowledge, to receive Him and His incarnational embrace and maintain His perfect work and occupy ourselves with the pursuit of the mysteries of serving Him as His Body on earth, the Sincere Church, in pursuit of the Mystery of Perfection as we perfect the saints for the work of this ministry as part of the Divine Plan.

If God poured out His wrath on Christ while He hung on a Cross on Calvary's hill as finished and perfected work for us, be assured that He will most certainly pour out His wrath on us if we die in our sins failing to pursue this mystery. The word is clear" He that believes not the Son shall not see life; but the wrath of God abides on Him' (John 3:36).

The Mystery of mysteries is God spared not His own Son when He took the sinner's place, nor will He spare the sinner who rejects the savior which is those who will not move forward into the pursuit of the mystery of perfection to delight themselves in Christ.

God himself must be the subject of our theology. The word "theology" comes from the Greek words *theos*, which means "God," and *logos*, which means "word." So, in the simplest sense, theology is the study of God's word, it also means the belief or study of what we believe about God. Therefore, Scripture alone is theology in the fullest sense of the word because it truly has God as its subject; it does not just speak of him but is His own Word. It is in the pages of the Biblical text that God comes lovingly to speak to us. It is in the study of the Bible that we seek to understand the mystery of His message of love and concern and grow in grace and knowledge of our Lord and Savior Jesus Christ and His saving grace (2 Peter 3:18).

God gave us His Word in order to deliver us from the power of the darkness of ignorance and to translate us into the domain of divine light, "the kingdom of the Son of His love" (Colossians 1:13). The bible reveals the mystery of the full scope of the Lord's redemptive plan for His people. This is the heart of wisdom and the mystery of perfection and His perfecting work and to the extent we pursue its truth we cannot walk in the ultimate truth and realm of light, life and love in the Lord Himself.

By pursuing the divine precepts and principles of the mystery of perfection revealed through scripture and pursued by sincere faith, a life of prayer, surrendered worship, fellowship of His suffering, and the power of divine grace as we partner with the Holy Spirit, we then position ourselves to receive the incarnational embrace of our Lord and Savior Christ the King. As we grow in grace and knowledge we gain the most important realm of all; that is: the ability to live a life under the dominion of His kingdom plan, presence, and power as we partner together in this Christ-life as a chosen people, a kingdom of priests and a holy nation, *"But you are not like that, for you are a chosen people. You are royal priests, a holy nation, God's very own possession. As a result, you can show others the goodness of God, for he called you out of the darkness into his wonderful light"* I Peter 2:9 NLT).

The bible does not tell us to live and learn because we are perfect but to learn and live as we grow and pursue the mystery of perfection through His grace and knowledge. The bible says; in Ephesians 4:12, we to be perfected for the work of the ministry as God's vehicle for bringing forth His kingdom. It progressively reveals the person, plan, character, mind, love and will of God as He perfects us in righteousness or right relationship with Him and each other as part of His divine plan.

The power of biblical knowledge is that it is the necessary path to righteousness. To seek intimate knowledge of God through the study of sacred Scripture can be compared to a journey, and like any journey it is important to have a roadmap to guide the traveler along the right path. Most fear is rooted in ignorance. Fear becomes for the one in search of the mystery of perfection like one who is lost without a map on the journey. As believers we are called to create the environment that determines people's moods in the environment of life, love, learning and leadership, and the mood we create as we pursue the ways of the Kingdom, in turn, affects productivity, possibility, partnerships as we move through levels of the passion of engagement with this mystery. Fear strangles our faith and hinders our pursuit of the mysteries of God. Our passion brings us into an intimate and personal relationship with God.

When we move the curtain of the mystery back a bit, we can see clearly that a person especially a leader's fear, bad mood, rebellion, doubt, disappointment and even disillusion is a source of infection – an emotional contagion that eventually spreads throughout the people one leads to the entire aspects of one's possibilities. The more knowledge or skill you have in any area, the less fear it holds. So, the mandate of the journey into the mystery of perfection is never stop learning and growing passionately or pursuing a relationship with God less purposely and fear not for God is with thee. The more you know about what you face, the clearer, more capable and committed the more conscious, courageous and confident you will be to face the challenges and move forward into the mystery of God's purposes and possibilities for your life.

Leadership guru Peter Drucker states: "Follow effective action with quiet reflection. From the quiet reflection will come effective action." From the ancient leadership lessons of Lao Tzu come this: "The leader is best when people are hardly aware of his existence, not so good when people praise his government, less good when people stand in fear, worst, when people are contemptuous. Fail to honor people, and they will fail to honor you. But a good leader, who speaks little when his work is done, his aim fulfilled, the people say, 'We did it ourselves." From the philosophy of the contemporary musical protégé Prince we have, "if you can't fully explain it, then you really can't do it."

The first step in the pursuit of the mystery is wisdom.

We pursue God only because He first put a passion within us that moves us forward toward the mystery of the wisdom of His perfection. "No man comes to Me except My Father draws them" said Jesus according to (John 6:44). The very impulse, or desire to pursue God begins with God, but the result of that desire is that we move ever forward drawn by His love, promise, power and purpose towards His mystery of perfection passionately.

All the time we are pursuing Him what we don't realize is that we have already been and always are in His hand. "My soul clings to you; your right hand upholds me" Psalm 63:8.

When it comes to having an intimate and personal relationship with God do you feel inadequate? Do you fear the unknown or unexplored? Is being with God more intentionally and intimately difficult, listening to Him and answering nearly improbable? Have we reduced God to what we have learned in the rather awkward and insufficient way we come to learn of God in church and not experience Him at new levels and dimensions of truth and passion? Has the mystery of God become mysterious and mindboggling as we grope through life not knowing how to actually become involved in the pursuit of the mystery of perfection itself? Which way do we go? What is true and what is false? What is real and what is just human imagination? Do I love Him as passionately as He has so sacrificially loved me and died on a Cross to prove it? Do I really want to pursue the mystery of perfection in Christ by dying to myself that I might live in Him?

Yet, Christ, His death, burial and resurrection remain a mystery to most. Confusing to many, and just plain foolishness to mainstream minds who think that they know it all and refuse to live, move and have their being at another realm of perfection as part of the dominion of God. After all, to pursue the mystery is to be in awe of God and His Christ. It means to give up control and submit ourselves to be led by God, dying to self and having our life, sense of being and purpose in the mystery of perfected-ness found in our pursuit of Christ.

We all come to a place where in moving forward we must realize there is far more to the Christian life than getting it right or knowing things about it. The pursuit of the mystery of perfection is in the living out of all aspects of our lives with clarity of purpose, confidence in God's capacity, commitment to the process, and consciousness of our gifting and calling as we move forward into and through the veil of promised perfection with passion for His glory and purpose.

Mostly, we know more about Scripture and truth than we do about how to live the life of faith through spiritually forming our souls in response to and in communication with God. Our souls, (our thinking, emotions and decisions) and our communication with God through prayer, preparation partnership, and purpose as a royal priesthood require the demands of the humility of our attention, as much as, the study of Scripture and truth. We must take seriously the life of the spirit even more so than the life of the mind and emotions without doubt, disappointment or delusion that give way to the life of the flesh which constantly cries out to be heard, to be dealt with and cared for.

But what about the relationship between the mystery of our souls in connection with the promise and the purpose of our spirits and life in Christ as we are perfected for kingdom work? Have we been sincerely taking the necessary path of righteousness as we live, move and have our being in Christ within our contemporary world? Is our true passion for the life of the Spirit or the life of the flesh? Is our pursuit of the life lived in Christ moving us boldly forward into the clarity, capacity, commitment and consciousness necessary to grow in grace and in knowledge of Christ and His purpose and kingdom perfection?

With these things in mind let's ground our thinking about the "The Mystery of Perfection", with this idea to guide us as we pursue it together: The Mystery of Perfection: *is the dignity of a life of prayer, the pursuit of intimacy with Christ, the purposeful submission to moving forward under the leading of the Holy Spirit, the grace of a fruitful existence in complete surrender in worship and wonder, and the reclaiming of the power and promise of the personal incarnational embrace of God through His word and action in our lives.*

Jesus preached a gospel of moving forward into the mystery of perfection, understood as the kingdom of God or God in perfected action. As God with us, Christ through the passion of His love, the purpose of the Father, and the power of the Holy Spirit, leads us into the mystery of perfection offering those who would pursue this mystery the availability and access to a life of grace and knowledge lived in Christ. This mystery has been available from the very beginning until now. It was revealed through the Good News of the death, burial and resurrection of Christ. Sadly however, we have reduced the mystery of this gospel of the kingdom, purpose of the plan, presence and power of the Trinity (the community of grace), and the purpose for the church (the community of faith), to solely being about forgiveness of sins and assurance of heaven.

This unfortunately is how many of those who have given their lives to Christ see the mystery as they come into the atmosphere and presentation of the church. They see the pursuit of perfection as a finish line instead of the start of a lifetime pursuit of the mystery of an eternal perfection bringing them into the kingdom of God to serve and do the work we are called to do. As a result, it has enormous implications for how we pursue and live this life.

Most people see Christianity as reaching a point of conversion and then see the call to become a disciple as a secondary level option reserved for more serious Christians. Scripture clearly indicates that the common reference for those who follow Jesus called disciples *(mathetes)* are understood as students, apprentices, or learners and appears 265 times in Scripture. Knowledge then is important in understanding and operating God's grace and perfect will. But it is not the most important. I would offer that it is an intimate and personal relationship with Christ that is paramount in encountering the mysteries of God. We have taken what we know about Christ and turned it into all we do for Christ, without being in intimate relationship with Christ and His purpose.

The word Christian by comparison is used just four times in the whole New Testament and when it is used it describes Jesus' followers by others. It is not even their word for their own relationship with Him but is the name used by those who would slight Him and condemn those who follow Him.

The term "Christian" over time became embraced by the community of faith as a badge of honor for being called "little Christ's." But understand it was how others saw them rather than how these followers saw themselves. This, though far from the same, is not unlike how the experience of the history of enslavement, colonization of our minds, methods and memories has caused Black people to embrace the negative descriptions of themselves with the use of the derogatory names we call each other. These names were first used on us and are now used by us and embraced as badges of honor by those who have become confused about what to call ourselves. Now we see the use Christian again is seen as negative and a metaphor for holy roller, churchy, fake, conservative, homophobic, insensitive, and a number of other things to identify those who should be seen as followers of Christ.

The way we have been called and seen as Christians in the last ten to twenty year's will not be how we call ourselves Christians in the next ten to twenty years. Some of you will become the Christians leaders in the next ten to twenty years. You need to be able to take a fresh look at scripture and offer with clarity, capacity, commitment and consciousness a fresh read of what God is saying to the world through Scripture in order to be people who can breath a fresh word out to the world in new ways. This must be done not by embracing the names the enemy calls us or what the frustrated among us assume but by the faith established through our pursuit of the mystery of God's perfection. Is how people see us as Christians still controlled by those talking about us rather than how we express our faith to them?

The mystery that must be understood and revealed is that the New Testament is a book about disciples, for disciples, by disciples as they pursued the mystery of perfection growing in grace and in knowledge as followers of Jesus Christ. We, as followers of Jesus Christ are called to live already in a world in which heaven and earth have come together. Let us seek to pursue the mysteries of this truth with clarity, capacity, commitment and consciousness and move forward into the mystery of perfection.

Beautiful Request

You asked me to be kind

To pray when in a bind

You asked me to stay true

To me and what I want to do

You asked me to use these gifts in which you gave me

And to do it for your glory

I promise to do my very best

To fulfill this beautiful request

___Zaina Goggins

Pursuing The Mystery of Perfection

1

GOD'S MYSTERIOUS PLAN

Paul writes in Colossians 1:24, "I am glad when I suffer for you in my body, for I am participating in the sufferings of Christ that continue for his body, the church." Christ personifies this plan. God's mysterious plan will be fulfilled. (Revelation 10:7)

The mystery of God is something understood but beyond our human understanding. It is a religious truth that one can know only by revelation and cannot fully be understood without the help and guidance of God.

Romans 11:25 says, "I want you to understand this mystery, dear brothers and sisters, so that you will not feel proud about yourselves." I Corinthians 2:7 further states regarding this mysterious plan: "The wisdom we speak of is the mystery of God – his plan that was previously hidden, even though he made it for our ultimate glory before the world began."

We are pursuing the mystery of perfection, speaking God's wisdom in a mystery which biblically refers to a truth previously hidden but now as we move forward into it – it is being revealed to us in the Good News of Christ and his saving work. (Romans 11:25-27; I Timothy 3:9, 16).

You and I must ask him to give us a clear image of the work he has called us to join him in accomplishing. So we see that perfection requires vision. It also requires clarity, capacity, commitment and spiritual consciousness. *Clarity* is reaching the Point of Biblically Defined Perception. *Capacity* is reaching the Point of Perfected Performance. *Commitment* is reaching the Point of Consistently Seeking Eternal Possibilities. *Consciousness* is reaching the Point of Purposeful Confidence in the Divine Plan.

A visionary person with clarity, capacity, commitment and consciousness understands that there is a calling and purpose in their life that needs to be pursued by Moving Forward, Pursing the Mystery of Perfection: Growing in Grace and In Knowledge.

Pursuing the Mystery!

WISDOM: The First Step In Pursuit of the Mystery of Perfection

While people seek knowledge about God, the challenge is a lack of understanding of the mysteries of God and the need to pursue intimacy. Knowledge precedes intellectual pursuits. Understanding derives from intimacy with that which is being pursued. That is why the scripture says in Proverbs 4:7: "Wisdom is the principal thing; therefore get wisdom: and with all thy getting get understanding."

The difference between knowledge and understanding can be seen in looking at those the Apostle Paul encountered in Colossae who mixed their belief with unbelief, their pursuit of knowledge without understanding.

Paul appears to have written the letter to address the dangerous heretical ideas and teaching which arose among the believers there. Paul attempts to correct incorrect teaching such as: (1) the need to observe Old Testament laws and ceremonies (Colossians 2:14, 20-23); (2) an emphasis on "deeper knowledge" only attainable to an elite few (Colossians 2:8-10, 18); (3) the worship of angels (Colossians 2:18) and; (4) an apparent denial of the deity of Christ (Colossians 1:15-17). Paul also gave attention to the distinction between our absolute equality in Christ (Colossians 3:11) yet preserving important God-established differences in roles (Colossians 3:18-4:1).

The Colossian heresy, "contained elements of what later became known as Gnosticism: that God is good, but matter is evil, that Jesus Christ was merely one of a series of emanations descending from God and being less than God (a belief that led them to deny His true humanity), and that a secret, higher knowledge above Scripture was necessary for enlightenment and salvation. Let's be perfectly clear that when we speak here about the mystery of perfection we are not speaking of mystery in this way.

So the Apostle Paul writes this letter to respond to this situation and to encourage the believers in their growth and pursuit of the mystery of perfection or in other words Christian maturity. Wisdom must be understood and is the first step in pursuit of this mystery.

Solomon writes in proverbs: "Wisdom is the principal thing; therefore get wisdom: and with all thy getting get understanding." What is wisdom? The word "wisdom" literally means having skill or capacity. Education will tell you how to do something, but wisdom will tell you why you ought to do something. And wisdom will also tell you when you ought to do something.

In other words, knowledge or education is the automobile, but wisdom is the fuel. Without wisdom you have no capacity to do what you may have knowledge to do. You have an automobile, it is pretty, expensive, has all the latest technology. But it just sits in the driveway collecting dust and bird excrement because you don't have any gas. This is how wisdom works in the pursuit of the mystery of perfection. Without the wisdom of pursing the mystery of God's perfection one will stall, stumble or even stop pressing toward the mark of a higher calling in Christ and become reduced to living a life of flesh, frustration and fantasy.

Wisdom is that supernatural edge that most people do not have, and have no idea how to get. King Solomon said: Wisdom is more valuable than gold, silver and rubies. In fact, if you don't have wisdom, you won't have and certainly won't keep much gold, silver and rubies. Could this be why most church folk are broke? Why so many of them seek prosperity messages and are fleeced by unscrupulous preachers and prosperity gurus making them rich while never attaining these riches for themselves? Could the issue be a lack of wisdom leading to fleshly desires, frustration, financial hardship and flights of fantasy for many?

Now very simply, here is the basic way to obtain true wisdom. But watch out: this is going to be so simple that you might miss it. What you have to do is ask God for it! That's right. Let's be perfectly clear about it. If you want true wisdom, you must simply ask God for it. You cannot work for wisdom; you cannot study and get wisdom; you cannot borrow wisdom; you cannot buy wisdom; and you cannot extract wisdom from other human beings. You can't even get it from your momma. The only way to get true wisdom is by simply praying and asking God for it. It is a free gift of the grace of God, as is your soul's salvation. *"If any of you lack wisdom, let him ask of God, that giveth to all men liberally, and upbraideth not; and it shall be given him."* (James 1:5)

The glorious wisdom that God gives will open your eyes to so many things that you cannot see right now. It opens the way to the pursuit of His perfect way, will and understanding through His Word. The wisdom of God will give you the ability to see things that the average person does not see. Having the wisdom of God will also definitely give you an advantage -- a great advantage in this life. God on your side! So I urge you to ask God for wisdom to guide you throughout your life, and He will do it for you.

If you want to be wise, it is wise to walk or hang out with wise men. King Solomon said: *"He that walketh with wise men shall be wise, but a companion of fools shall be destroyed."* - Proverbs 13:20

So many today walk with foolish people, foolish ideas about life, love and what leads to destiny. Misery loves company but so it seems do fools and I might add so-called mature Christians. Being in church doesn't qualify for wisdom. Being with God and walking with wise people certainly places one on the path.

Here are some other quotes from those whose pursuit of wisdom brought them to a place called understanding.

- "The world belongs to the man who is wise enough to change his mind in the presence of facts." Roy L. Smith

- "Patience is bitter but its fruit is sweet." Jean Jacques Rousseau

- "Gentlemen, try not to become men of success. Rather, become men of value." Albert Einstein

- "Perhaps the most valuable result of all education is the ability to make yourself do the thing you have to do, when it ought to be done, whether you like it or not." Unknown

- The tragedy of life doesn't lie in not reaching your goal. The tragedy lies in having no goal to reach. It isn't a calamity to die with dreams unfilled, but it is a calamity not to dream." Dr. Benjamin Mays

- "... the circumference of life cannot be rightly drawn until the center is set." Dr. Benjamin Mays
- "Every man and woman is born into the world to do something unique and something distinctive and if he or she does not do it, it will never be done." Dr. Benjamin Mays
- "Not failure, but low aim is sin." Dr. Benjamin Mays
- "When love is lost, do not bow your head in sadness; instead keep your head up high and gaze at the stars for that is where your broken heart has been sent to heal!" Unknown
- "In life, there is no pause button, no rewind, and definitely no replay" Unknown
- "When I let go of what I am, I become what I might be" Lao Tzu
- "Don't ask what the world needs. Ask what makes you come alive, and go do it. Because what the world needs is people who have come alive." Howard Thurman
- "There is something in every one of you that waits and listens for the sound of the genuine in yourself. It is the only true guide you will ever have. And if you cannot hear it, you will all of your life spend your days on the ends of strings that somebody else pulls." Howard Thurman
- "Commitment means that it is possible for a man to yield the nerve centre of his consent to a purpose or cause, a movement or an ideal, which may be more important to him than whether he lives or dies." Howard Thurman

➢ At the core of life is a hard purposefulness, a determination to live." Howard Thurman

VISION: The Next Step in Pursing the Mystery of Perfection

It is impossible to properly lead people into the mysteries of God without a well-defined vision. Vision sets a mark in the Spirit toward which people can work. If it is missing or confused, then the people have no ability to adequately define their calling, ministries or to receive a proper vision of their own purpose or promises. Disunity of the body and lack of positive direction are the consequence.

What is commonly called vision in the Church today is often little more than a business plan by church leaders for the promotion of their ministries and churches according to worldly standards, disassociated from the processes and purposes of God. Even visions that come from the mind of man can produce worldly success (numbers, money, notoriety) within the church. These types of visions usually speak of the call of God in a leader to win the city or the nation, even the entire world for Christ.

A vision from God in which the sincere church can find biblical order is something mysteriously quite different from this disunity spoken of above. To lead requires vision. It also requires clarity, capacity, commitment and spiritual consciousness.

In some ways, we can say that wisdom is the God-given ability to see the true nature of things. In addition to everlasting life with him, God gives us a new way of looking at things in the here and now. He gives us the ability to see things as they really are, to see truth and not merely facts. By the power of the indwelling Holy Spirit, the blinders are taken off so that we can see temporary things in light of eternity. God gives us the gift of vision, and his vision allows us to see the mystery of His perfection in our present reality in light of eternity.

Few things are more important to effectively living a life of perfected promise than vision. Good leaders foresee something out there, vague as it might appear from the distance that others don't see. Godly leaders who are followers of Christ must first have a vision of who God is and the future he holds for them. They must also have a sense of what God has called them to do.

The apostle Paul had both. Through a miraculous vision, he was taken into heaven where he saw images too spectacular to communicate; images he wasn't allowed to communicate: "I must go on boasting. Although there is nothing to be gained, I will go on to visions and revelations from the Lord. I know a man in Christ who fourteen years ago was caught up to the third heaven. Whether it was in the body or out of the body I do not know – God knows. And I know that this man – whether in the body or apart from the body I do not know, but God knows – was caught up to paradise. He heard inexpressible things, things that man is not permitted to tell. I will boast about a man like that, but I will not boast about myself, except about my weaknesses. Even if I should choose to boast, I would not be a fool, because I would be speaking the truth. But I refrain, so no one will think more of me than is warranted by what I do or say."(2 Corinthians 12:1-6)

Paul was given a vision into the mystery of perfection from God – a vision that enabled him to withstand trials and temptations without giving up or giving in. But there was a second vision Paul possessed.

The first was of heaven's mystery of perfection and his future home. The second was a vision of his earthly ministry revealed among the imperfections of the Corinthians. He knew God had called him to minister to the Gentiles (Romans 1:15). And he knew that the Lord was directing him to return to the Corinthians a third time. In Romans he also spoke about the mystery of his perfected pursuit, his vision to take the gospel to Rome and Spain (Romans 15:23-24).

While God may not give you a vision of the mystery of perfection in heaven like Paul experienced, or even like John, who was taken up into heaven in Revelations, He will however, not fail to give you one of Himself. Through his Word, He will show you what He is like and will give you insight into your spiritual destiny through purpose, preparation, prayer, partnership as His priesthood. As you seek Him through his Word and through prayer, ask him to show you Himself.

Meditation . . .

MOVING FORWARD:
PURSUING THE MYSTERY OF PERFECTION

In moving forward, many of us must recognize what has so often held us back and had us walking in place for so long. Many get overtaken by life and run back to what is familiar and what they perceive as secure. Others are paralyzed by fear of the unknown. The claimed unknown only occurs when one stops his pursuit and reflects a faulty witness that reveals that he does not know God the Father, has no relationship with Jesus Christ the Son, and has never surrendered to the power of the Holy Spirit.

We serve a God like no other---one that claimed his love for us before we recognized Him at all. God's mission and plan is above all our thoughts could ever comprehend but we must move forward and apprehend what's apprehended us. Pursue the mystery of perfection, truly longing and striving to be Christ-like. Jesus is the way, the truth, and the life. (John 14:6) We must stand on his Word and be determined that there is no other life to lead but one that is passionately, searching, seeking, chasing, and living according to His purpose.

Moving forward on the Highway of Perfection as authentic followers of Christ has led to the need to focus on four goals--- CLARITY, CAPACITY, COMMITMENT, AND CONFIDENCE

CLARITY... God's Presence, Expression of Pleasure, and Purpose in the faithful Interpretation of God's Word

In the beginning, God created the heavens and the earth. Now the earth was formless and empty, darkness was over the surface of the deep, and the Spirit of God was hovering over the surface. And God said, "Let there be light." God saw that light was good and separated the light from the darkness. **Genesis 1:1-4**

Let us make man in our image, after our likeness and let them have dominion over all the earth, and over every creeping thing that creepeth upon the earth. So God created man in his own image, in the image of God created he him; male and female created he them. And God blessed them, and God said unto them, Be fruitful, and multiply, and replenish the earth, and subdue it; and have dominion over the fish of the sea, and over the fowl of the air, and over every living thing that moveth upon the earth. **Genesis 1:26-28**

God as Creator of the Heavens and the earth is one of the undeniable beliefs of Christians. As soon as we compromise on this belief, we then start questioning 'Is there truly a God?' 'How does He speak?' 'What is His will for my life?'

We've all heard the saying, if you want to know someone's future, you must first start with one's beginning (paraphrased). Moving forward in clarity requires a faithful interpretation of God's Word.

In the beginning God was present and His Spirit hovered as He contemplated His divine plan. In the beginning, God, the Father among the Holy Trinity, created with all magnificence and glory. He set every celestial body in place and carved out landforms. In the beginning, God had a place for himself and those whom he created to love and love Him. In the beginning, His voice was heard throughout the universe clearly revealing his omnipotence. 'Let there be' was proclaimed and God's plan was set in motion. The Lord articulated his intentions and his pleasure as He separated light from darkness. His divine plan was to continue that separation in all that He created. God saw that light was good and expressed His pleasure.

Any denial of the Creation would mean dismissing God's presence, muting His voice that proclaims His will and way to His children, and stifling any motivation to seek out what truly pleases Him. Moving forward is simply knowing that God is the beginning and the end, and His will - will be done through us in the mean time.

God has been clear since the very origin of man. Men and women are to rule, multiply, and replenish the earth. *Let there be* all that God created to do so in his image. We are to live like sons and daughters of the king. Living lives full of possibilities and passion to be all that God intended. As light and salt, we expose the wicked, shine in the darkest of situations, change the atmosphere and preserve God's vision of hope and love in the earth empowered by the connection to the Son commanded to bear fruit and go into the world making disciples in His name.

Dear Father God,

How excellent is Your Name O Lord! You have set your glory above the heavens. When I ponder how You have considered all things from the very beginning, Lord I cannot fathom Your works. What is man that you are mindful of him? You made him a little lower than You O God and yet you crowned him with glory and honor. You made him ruler over all that You have created.

Lord God, knowing that You the Father, the Son, and the Holy Spirit have been present since the beginning brings clarity to Your intended purpose for my life. You created me and commanded in that I take authority over all that You have set in my atmosphere. I shall not be overwhelmed by any obstacles in my way but name them and make 'Let there be' proclamations allowing the light of your Word to illuminate my path and guide my feet.

Your presence has empowered me to fulfill Your most excellent plans. Your Spirit guides and comforts me along the way. Your Son has made me free from the bondage of mistakes, missteps, and the misappropriation of my gifts. I take authority of any uncertainty in my life through the truth I find in Your Word. I am fully aware that You love me and created me to love and honor You with my life. O Lord, I am humbled by Your thoughts of me. O God, 'Let there be' your presence in my life. 'Let there be' good pleasure that You find in me. 'Let there be' purposeful and passionate pursuit of Your mysteries for the rest of my life. In Jesus' Holy Name, Amen.

Danielle Osonduagwuike

CLARITY: Reaching the Point of Biblically Defined Perspective

Clarity is reaching the Point of Biblically Defined Perceptive. "So if the Son sets you free, you are truly free (John 8:36). It is where you can say "When I think of the goodness of Jesus and all that He has done for me, my soul cries hallelujah, thank you Jesus for saving me." Perspective is everything. You mustn't look at your challenges and agree with the difficulty surrounding them. You have to look at attacks and challenges differently. You can't look to the world for Godly perspective and purpose. You must pursue the mystery of Godly perfection and maintain your biblically defined perspective according to the clarity of kingdom purpose, power and plan.

Life's challenges are not supposed to paralyze you they're supposed to propel you to keep moving forward and help you discover who you truly are. Help you gain a biblically defined perspective. There are two very powerful biblical challenges that should provoke you in the search for their true meanings and intended applications. They are the words:

1. "Man was made in God's image."
2. "The Truth will set you free."

These two challenges are very inter-connected in the pursuit of the mystery of perfection and help us to gain a biblically defined perspective.

With the first challenge, "Man was made in God's image" we appear to see a clearer picture of the meaning, but I think we may have stumbled upon the real intention of the original challenge as we pursue the deeper clarity of this mystery—which is to understand what part of "image' is it that we most as believers resemble God. And the most important part of the image is the awesome power of belief. Over and over again God has proven the power of His belief in us using our free will to eventually do the right thing—love God and love one another. Granted, it takes some of us a little longer to get to this image of what we should be, but eventually we who believe all do.

Belief is an unconscious code shaped in the pursuit of the mystery of perfection where we speak back to God what we believe He has revealed through His Word. It is a combination of thoughts and feelings that project their energy back to the universe without the normal human verbal opportunity for miscommunication. Beliefs are communication at its best. There is clarity with no misunderstanding, no miscommunication or no misinterpretation in the translation.

The Question in belief is: which part don't you believe? What are you unclear about? It is what it is. God said it, and I believe its truth, so I faithfully communicate it by clearly repeating His Word, by my Walk and the Wise Witness of the Holy Spirit's spiritual guidance and direction as I live, move and have my being pursuing the mystery of perfection.

Clarity is reaching the Point of Biblically Defined Perceptive. When looking at the point of clearly defined perspective we can look at Moses as he recorded 613 instructions given to him by God as he led God's people forward into the presence of God and the mystery of perfection. These 613 instructions were given to him to reach a clearly defined perspective of what God wanted from His people.

The scriptures tell us that ten were heard by the entire congregation of Israel gathered at Mt Sinai, the Mountain of God as they pursued the mystery of perfection after being delivered from bondage in Egypt. Egypt being a representation of the world system, we see that God gave instructions for living the life of this mystery He was freely offering by His authority.

The Decalogue or the Ten Commandments of God were written onto tablets of stone by the very finger of God. The finger was an idiom to mean "the authority of God." So God wrote out His instructions and placed them in Moses hand to instruct the people who were to be brought to God by Moses to worship Him and live out God's promised life.

The Decalogue or the Ten Commandments of God provides one of the best systems for categorizing and communicating these 613 instructions into the Word which is what Jewish people call the Torah and Christians call the first five books of Moses (Genesis, Exodus, Leviticus, Numbers, and Deuteronomy). On two tablets, God listed His divine perspective broken down for clarity into ten of these instructions. The first five Commandments instructed mankind about the mystery of our relationship with God. The last five Commandments instructed mankind about our relationship with one another. The first five give us a clear vision of God's image, the next five offers clarity for how the truth sets us free to live fully redeemed lives by the image revealed once received faithfully.

This is the heart of what God is saying: that you take the 613 instructions of God, and break them down into the two tablets of the Ten Commandments to gain biblically defined perspective. All

613 fall within these two tablets; five instructions are about our relationship with God, and five relate to our relationship with one another. Through these we gain the clarity we need to move forward into the mystery of perfection. Again, I ask the question of belief: which part don't you clearly understand?

In essence these two tablets are like two witnesses liken unto Moses and Elijah (Revelation 11:3). Satan tried his best to destroy the Word of God, but God has anointed His Holy scriptures, in this case the two tablets written by His authority, 'the two anointed ones', and no matter how small a flame the truth of God's Word flickers through our neglect or ignorance, Satan will never be able to put it out, because of our witness of the Truth and clarity of our biblically defined perspective.

When Christians say that these two wise witnesses are Moses and Elijah, they are not completely wrong. You see, Moses and Elijah represent the mystery of perfection through the Word of God. Moses represents the Law and Elijah represents the Prophets. Jesus gives us clarity when He confirmed that He did not come to destroy the law and the prophets, but to fulfill them. The word "fulfill" meaning; "to exalt," "to bring a clearer understanding" or in a word offer clarity. As we know, Moses and Elijah are in Heaven. We know this because they appeared with Jesus on the mount of transfiguration.

Exodus 20:1-2 says, "And God spoke these words, saying "I AM the Lord your God, who brought you out of the Land of Egypt, out of the house of bondage." What is interesting about this text is that there has been some manipulation of this text by some of the believing bodies over the years, because we like things to be neat and orderly. But this text does not fall into the easy "you shall", or the "you shall not" categories we like. So over time there has been a subtle changing of the text.

This, however, shows the first command. It is simply God saying "I AM the Lord your God," the One who took you out of Egypt out of the house of bondage."

So here is the First Commandment:

1. I am the Lord your God – (Exodus 20:2)
2. You shall not recognize the gods of others in My presence" (Exodus 20:3).

God laid out His commands in chronological order so we could reach the point of clarity as we seek to understand and comprehend His mystery of perfection. We believe there is a flow to the spiritual direction offered by the Holy Spirit that happens when you commit to how God has laid out these commands in the Scriptures. There is a mystery to His perfection and an order in His process. To its clarity we must become committed. We believe that this was the intent of God. If we are to grow in His grace and knowledge we must have clarity about the need to pursue this mystery reaching the point of clarity.

Under each of the Ten Commandments we soon discover that in each category you can find the 613 instructions. Under the first one, 42 of the 613 fall under this category: "I am the LORD your God." When you read them something very interesting comes out where God will give a positive and a negative one right after the other.

He'll say, "I Am the Lord your God who took you out of the Land of Egypt" and then say, "you shall not recognize the gods of others in My presence." Your mouth shall not cause their names to be heard." He couples the positive perspective to give clarity along with the negative and causes a greater emphasis to each instruction as the Lord spoke it and as we clearly pursue His mystery of perfection.

"You shall," He said, and the truth is that you'll find yourself doing it and when you find yourself doing it, you'll know that I AM has been there. When you are clear I have been there you'll fall to your knees and praise God for being your I AM. And you'll say 'thank God for what He was doing instead of what you are trying to do. This is reaching the biblically defined point of perspective. You know when God has been there. You know when God is there. You have faith that I AM will be there.

In reality, if we try to do it in our flesh we can't accomplish it, it'll be death. Which is the reason why so many people don't even attempt to do what God says anymore? They think this is too overwhelming that they're under the Law negatively. When the truth is you and I are no longer under the Law of sin and death, but under the mystery of the perfect love of Christ Jesus and the community of grace, known as His sincere church, of which Christ is the head and we are His body.

Christ has made us the end of the Law, which is seen by the wearing of the tallis or strings which hang from the Jewish prayer shawls. Do we see the clarity in all this yet? Or is it all too hard to believe? These are the goals that will point you to the need for Christ and our pursuit of His perfect way, will and Word. These strings are hanging from the prayer shawl to remind us of His way, His instructions.

With one look at all the commandments we knew who couldn't do them all. We couldn't get through one day without breaking one of these commandments so they are represented as the tallis or strings hanging from the prayer shawls worn by the Jewish rabbis and now popular in praying Christian communities to remind us. We wear these prayer shawls but are we clear about what they represent?

So understanding the mystery of all this could be so paralyzing for the people, where they realized that here was the Lord saying "I know you can't keep them." That's why I have a plan if you will pursue the mystery of perfection that will enable you to do it by My Spirit so that God gets the glory and not you.

Further, He will bridge the gap when we fall short. God is not saying that we are going to walk out these commands or instructions for life and do them all perfectly, which was the legalistic approach even at the critical religious point of approaching all this for the Jewish people. God was saying even if you try and fall short I will bridge the gap to the lack of perfection and perspective in your attempts to do it.

So God wants us to go for it, give it shot, make the attempt to pursue the mystery of perfection. To press forward in our clear need to reach the point of biblically defined perspective. Passionately, we are to go after the wisdom of God. The only difference between one season and another season in your life is the wisdom contained in the mystery of God through His Word. Why sit in one season of your life and stay stuck there without going forward into the possibilities of another season of your life because you refuse the wisdom of God or the command to move forward until you are clear about what God has for you?

This is what happened as Moses was bringing the children of Israel to God and out of the bondage they had endured for years. You and I should want the wisdom of God as we come to grow in grace and knowledge so passionately that we're compelled to move forward in the mystery of another level of God's perfected wisdom.

3. Make no mention of the name of other gods,. (Exodus 23:13)
4. neither let it be heard out of thy mouth (Exodus 23:13)

The contexts of these instructions are important to the clarity of the pursuit of the mystery of perfection and biblically defined perspective also. God offers things line upon line, precept upon precept to highlight certain things as He repeats them at certain times in our lives. The first commandment may stand out for you for a certain season of your life. But It would be important then to see what are the other things of wisdom being offered by God's instruction as you reach the point of biblically defined perspective in another season of my life.

I can memorize 'I AM the Lord your God." But what does that look like as I walk that out in pursuit of the mystery of perfection daily? As you walk this out every day here is what God says, reach the point of clarity and "Don't mention the gods of others in My presence; " 'Don't let your mouth cause those names to be heard" as you move forward growing in grace and in knowledge of Me. So as we pursue the mystery of perfection daily and reach certain points of biblically defined perspective God gives us practical instructions of His wisdom (God's Clarity). Without the practical application my conduct is not going to match my confession. So I come to the point of a divine biblical perspective as I encounter and receive the wisdom of God through His practical instruction daily.

Exodus 20:3-5 'You shall have no other gods before ME. You shall not make yourself a carved image nor any likeness of that which is in the heavens.... above or on the earth below or in the water beneath the earth. You shall not prostrate yourself to nor worship them, for I am the Lord your ... God – a jealous God."

If you have a legalistic mindset all you see is "you shall not." You shouldn't be doing that or better yet, you'll find yourself not doing it by the desires of God. It is very critical that we let the Holy Spirit lead us because it is not only by the letter of the Law or the Word that we gain this perspective but the Word and the Spirit. It is the Holy Spirit's guidance that balances our correct interpretation of the Word and gives us clear biblically defined perspective.

Under the second command, "You shall not make for yourself carved images" (Exodus 20:4). "You shall not bow down to carved images" (Exodus 20:5). We can become word terrorist and grab things out of context and just say we are not to have these things . . . carved images for example. So home we go with a hammer to smash all of the images and statues we find in our homes and lives, photographs, things on the television and in our children's rooms or relationships with friends and anything that we perceive as a graven or manmade image and feel like it is our job to get rid of them.

But what this does in the pursuit of the mystery of perfection is remove this command from the context in which God spoke it.

The context in which God spoke this is 'Look you are coming out of all this stuff, when you were in Egypt (or the world) and you really didn't know who I was God says; this stuff was really quite common to you. This is not strange or unfamiliar stuff to you. You came out in the exodus from a place where you had a lot of gods, ideas, addictions, money, sex, lust, greed, profanity, ego, prejudice, cursing and bondage. You used to party, now you want to judge dancing in church like it is from the devil. No! Don't dance in church like you are still in the club, or in other words don't drop it. . . like it's hot!' Dance unto the Lord like David for example. Though the Scripture says he danced (and his wife said he was naked) it only implies he was unashamed of worshiping God. Don't accuse your child of doing what you yourself have done. But praise God for deliverance and trust in the Lord and lean not to your own understanding. Do not lock your child into the prison of your regrets or even your neglect.

Contextually, this is still foreign to us today. But when we look at what God delivered you from, your gods might have been 'pornography; they might have been alcohol; they might have been drug addiction; they might have been womanizing; they might have been promiscuity.

What God is saying is "don't put those things before you." That would be a trap for you. Don't make your mouth cause those things to be heard. Don't dwell on them. Don't look at them. Don't do advertizing about them by hanging them on your refrigerator or making them a screen saver on your computer. Don't have a picture of your ex- secretly in your wallet or in your nightstand draw or a secret file hidden away in your cell phone or communicating with them via Facebook. Don't keep her name in your cell phone (Tiger). Do let a pimp or your partners bring you no teenage girls (like former NFL player Lawrence Taylor), and you need to stay away from college girls (Ben Rothlisberger who is the quarterback of the Steelers). Don't kill dogs for fun and lose millions and jeopardize your whole career because you want to impress your friends (Michael Vick). What goes on in Vegas you can't do O.J! This kind of behavior will cost you. Don't take your bad decisions out on your child. Don't continue to do things at the age of 40 with the same goals and perspective you had at age 16. Grow up, mature, gain perspective move into the mystery of Godly perfection.

Though there are no absolutes in the world only in the spiritual realm. The closest might be this however: it is true nothing good happens at 3:00am in a strip club. As the creator of the African American celebration of Kawanzaa, Dr. Maulana Karenga is fond of saying, 'if you stay too long in a whore house you are bound at some time to turn a trick."

It is not that the gods of Egypt don't have any power. When Moses made his staff into a snake, the magic men of Egypt were able to do the same thing. The gods of Egypt or the world do have power. Now the truth of the matter is that God was stronger. But you can look at an old ancient idol and think "how can anyone fall down and worship that if you are foolish enough to think that way?

Yet, they in turn could look at us and say how can you worship certain brands of "beer' as they are presented in TV advertisements every day just because some pretty woman is advertizing it. How can you fall down under the power of another spirit; alcohol, meth, cocaine, crack . . . to become intentionally drunk, high, addicted, sprung, cracked out? How can someone have so much power over your life that you will allow them to beat the hell out of you while you believe that it is only because they love you so much. That is what happens when we think the gods of Egypt or the world have no power. They just are not stronger than God. But the truth is they are stronger than you, so God says don't put those things before you, don't allow them to hang out with you. Don't call them up and for God sake don't allow yourself to schedule a 'oh what the hell" night with them.

When we look at Exodus 20 – there is an image of an owl which represents the god Molech in Leviticus. "Thou shalt not give of thy seed to cause to pass through the fire for Moloch." (Leviticus 18:21)

The Bible does not attempt to prove the existence of demons any more than it attempts to prove the existence of God. It simply reports on their activities as if its first readers accepted their existence. Nor did the early church fathers have a problem with the reality and personality of demons. Origen wrote: "In regard to the devil and his angels and opposing powers, the ecclesiastical teaching maintains that the beings do indeed exist; but what they are or how they exist is not explained with sufficient clarity.

Molech: "A detestable national god of the Ammonites (I Kings 11:7) was worshiped by Israel in times of desertion and departure from the faith according to 2 Kings 23:10; and expressed by the sacrifice of children, in which they were caused to pass through or into the fire. Palestinian excavations have uncovered evidences of infant skeletons in burial places around heathen shrines. Ammonites revered Molech as a protecting father. Worship of Molech was stringently prohibited by Hebrew law. (Lev. 18:21; 20:1-5) Solomon built an altar to Molech. Manasseh in his idolatrous orgy also honored this deity. Josiah desecrated the Hinnom Valley altar, but Jehoiakim revived the cult." Molech was worshiped because it was associated with sexual sins including child sacrifice.

We are undone in this society by the continuous sexual exploits of our leaders both in and out of the pulpit , church, and homes with the abandonment, abuse and abortion of our children to be sacrificed on the altars of ungodly homes, communities, and exploited by unsaved churches and pedophiliac priests, pastors, and teachers, while they're subjected daily to uncommitted schools and overwhelmed and undermined teachers, juvenile court and the industrial prison complex systems that builds itself on the self fulfilling prophecies of failed homes, schools, churches and communities, internet predators, gangs, guns, drugs and dummies. Daily our children are walking into and being sacrificed in the fires of the day, hot lust, hot lead, hot heads, hot words, heated situations, and the fires of their own desires.

Even our children's peer group will use social networks like Facebook, twitter, text messaging etc., to destroy the lives of their school mates and friends as they neglect to care about each other's character, health or promise and let jealousy, envy and slander ruin the futures of young lives daily with their words and actions as they worship on the altar of today's Molech.

Is it really still true that sticks and stones may break your bones but words can never hurt you? Ask those children who have been destroyed by listening to the power in words offered on the unscrupulous altar of internet society networking systems of our day that influence them to commit atrocities of unmentionable dimensions and the sacrifice of countless lives by those whose promise from God was to have life more abundantly. Ask the young girls (and I might add, young boys too) who are being abducted, molested, raped and murdered everyday as they are enticed by both family members, friends and predators by comforting words that soon turn deadly as they're thrown in the fire and sacrificed.

How many desecrations have occurred on the altar of Molech established in homes that worship at the altars of arguments, abortions, abusive behavior, abandonment and adultery? How many children have be abducted by pain, and delivered through promiscuity to diseases and death, destroyed by loneliness, hindered by the history of hurt, and have had their lives broken by generational cures and disfigured by just the plain lack of parenting?

How many people have been affected by an adversarial spirit turning them into monsters who roam our communities terrorizing it because of the hopelessness and despair that has led them to believe they have no other options? They've been disfigured by the fires of this Molech worshipping generation.

How much has evil spirits, demons and the devil himself created dark spaces and darkened places for our children to become dis-spirited, apathetic, suicidal, chronically depressed, and disillusioned about church, their own promises offered by living out their destiny pursuing the mystery of the Christ-life?

The opinion held by most is that the devil was an angel; and having rebelled against God, he persuaded as many angels as possible to fall away with him; and these, even to the present time, are called his angels. Every day we walk the painful path of seeing our angels in hospitals, drug rehab facilities, court rooms, foster homes, prison cells, and cemeteries.

Luke 11:24-26 gives us a helpful view into the personality and individuality of evil spirits. We can glean several points of information about evil spirits from it. Demons can exist outside or inside humans. They are able to travel. They are able to communicate. Each one has a separate identity. They are able to remember and make plans. They are able to evaluate and make decisions. They are able to combine forces. They vary in degrees of wickedness.

But let's be clear, you need not fear Satan and his demons as long as you cling to God's truth and are determined to pursue the mystery of God's perfecting promises. Their only weapon is deception. Irenaeus wrote, "The devil . . . can only go to this length, as he did at the beginning, to deceive and lead astray the mind of man into disobeying the commandments of God, and gradually to darken the hearts." If you continue to walk in the light, you don't need to be afraid of the darkness. Be not deceived

God cares for each us and wants us to pursue the words and ways of Jesus and not this Molech loving world.

My prayer is, "Lord, thank you for revealing this to us because we have a lot of Molech gods, evil spirits, and demonic forces in our lives looking over the churches, homes, schools and entire cities of the nation, and we have created some Molech gods ourselves. Thank you for freeing us; and continuously causing us to walk out our lives in you; under the clarity of your commandments; and under the inspiration and direction of the Holy Spirit. You are a great God, greatly to be praised and we just want to serve you and the mystery of your majestic perfection."

Looking back at the list of commandments again, we see "I Am the Lord thy God and you shall have no other gods before me." The clarity of this is that in your pursuit of the mystery of perfection you will find that you won't have any other gods before you – when you discover with clarity God's community of grace called His sincere church. I know we continuously discover religion but have we encounter the sincere church of Christ, where He is the head and we as we gather become His body for His glory?

When I am wrestling with false images, religious icons and fake personalities that are trying to pull me down, I remember my commitment to the command that I shall have no other gods before thee. I will add, no personality shall hinder the clarity of your presence in my life and my personal pursuit of an intimate and personal relationship with You. You and You alone are my God. You are more powerful than these things that want to deceive and destroy me.

How is it that God can gather us and re-gather us back to the land of His promise and the mystery of His perfection as we assemble weekly in His church without clarity? Let's be clear that the way he brought the Word to you - was prophecy. Prophecy is speaking clearly "what thus saith the Lord."

Isaiah 29:9 says, "With my soul have I desired thee in the night; yea, with my spirit within me will I seek thee early: for when thy judgments are in the earth, the inhabitants of the world will learn righteousness.

God's prophesy in Isaiah 54 says I will come to you by My Spirit and I'll bring you my commands, I will write them on your hearts and mind. I will reveal them to you while you are in the midst of all these things around you that are trying to destroy you. I will stretch out my hand and the finger of God (my authority) and bring you out of that and bring you to a higher level with God, into biblically defined perspective leading you to the mystery of perfection. You'll look back and be freed of it all to pursue the mystery of perfection and live a fully redeemed life in Christ.

But, timing is everything in pursing the mystery of perfection and there is always a point of biblical perspective when we are more open to realizing the critical crossroads where we have to be at in order to begin making the right choices before we go past the point of no return without catching it in time. The crossroads we all come to is the one where we confront the reality of whether or not we are truly happy and successful from the choices we have made and the efforts we have put forth to progress in our journeys with the gift of our genetic capacity being made in God's image. It is at this point of divine biblical perspective that the truth that can set us free moves from: "No not yet," forward to "Yes starting right now."

The Spirit of God continues in so many tangible ways to reveal new levels of commitment and truth to us that it would be a shameful expression of our faith and fidelity to this calling we have as a sincere church to go on ignoring the clear signs God is sending to us regarding the mystery of perfection, the perfecting of the saints and the perfecting promise on our lives and ministry as we pursue the Truth.

Prophetically, God was saying in the Book of Jonah - Jonah, be perfectly clear about this, I want you to go to Nineveh, the difficult place, the place where you will have to give up your way of doing things and fight the good fight of faith, in the place called Nineveh, which means "evil or disaster." You are to go were evil (or life lived in opposition to grace and truth) has placed a stronghold on people's lives and faith hindering their ability to move forward in pursuit of God's purpose and plan and where people have aligned themselves with things that will only bring them down and cause disaster through their choices, challenges and conflicts with His calling on their lives.

After years of neglect, denial, and disobedience, it is clarity that brings you and God's purpose for your life to the crossroads of decision, a place where you have to use your faith or lose it. Tarshish in the story of Jonah is the place where we can decide to go in the opposite direction away from the presence of the Lord because we don't want to be obedient to His purpose. Which when viewed from our point of witness shows that with each step we take away from pursuit of the mystery of perfection and the presence of the Lord takes us one step closer to "going down to death" - the death of our faith in God, death of our faith in His church, death of our faith in our ministries and the faith we have in the hope of our calling.

We cannot afford any longer to turn away from the presence of the Lord as He instructs and perfects us to do the work of the ministry He has called us to be accountable for. He will hold each of us accountable for the choices we make and the chances we take with His purpose for our lives. Will you go where God tells you to go and do exactly what He says or will you go in the opposite direction and risk . . . going down? It is time for clarity as we faithfully carry out the call on our lives.

Meditation . . .

CAPACITY...to Experience the Endless Possibilities of God

*After his sufferings, he showed himself to these men and many convincing proofs that he is alive. He appeared to them over a period of forty days and spoke about the kingdom of God. On one occasion, while he was eating with them, he gave them the command; "Do not leave Jerusalem, but wait for the gift my Father promised, which you have heard me speak about. For John baptized with water but in a few days you will be baptized with the Holy Spirit. So when they met together, they asked him, "Lord, are you at this time going to restore the kingdom to Israel? He said to them "it is not for you to know the times of dates the Father has set by his own authority. But you will receive power when the Holy Spirit comes on you; and you will be my witnesses in Jerusalem and in Judea and Samaria and to the ends of the earth." **Acts 1:3-8***

When the day of Pentecost came, they were all together in one place. Suddenly a sound like the blowing of a violent wind came from heaven and filled the whole house where they were sitting. They saw what seemed to be tongues of fire that separated and came to rest on each of them. All of them were filled with the Holy Spirit and began to speak in other tongues as the Spirit enabled them. **Acts 2:1-4**

Capacity, can be defined as capability, competence, and the ability to receive. In moving forward on this Christian journey, where does one gain the capacity or the ability to receive all that God has for him? How does a Christian increase in his capacity to move faithfully in the faith and integrity of God and fulfill the call to righteousness?

The disciples walked closely with Jesus. The forty days Jesus taught them after His resurrection gave them confidence and increasing enthusiasm to spread the gospel. Jesus commanded the disciples not to leave Jerusalem but to wait for the gift that God, the Father, had promised them about which he also had been teaching. How many times has God told you to be still but by your own might, you decided to move? Did you hear his voice telling you to stay faithful in fellowship so that you could be strengthened through worship and the confirmation of His Word? How often have you denied God your time and held back your presence from Him and your brothers and sisters in Christ? How can God continue the perfecting process when all you want to do is leave when it gets difficult?

God has given us many natural examples to show us why the process of waiting, gathering, pressing, and heating is necessary to developing what will last. The finest wine is made by an intricate process of choosing specific grapes and sending it through a series of pressing and refining processes. The wine can last years and gets more valuable over time as it sits in wait to be used. The finest gold is found in unexpected places in the earth and sent through extreme heat and pressure situations just so its owner can use it for many- many years. Diamonds are created by closely packed atoms, found in the depths of the earth, and can withstand up to 1400 degrees Celsius. Diamonds are used for many purposes, from jewelry to the most essential parts of heavy machinery. Diamonds have the capacity to cut, grind, drill, and polish the most rigid and hard surfaces yet can shine brightly enough to adorn kings and queens. Yet, man-made diamonds are pretty but don't have the potential and power as those made and found naturally in God's creation.

If God can create such elements for the use of man, do you not realize what the power and fire of His Holy Spirit can develop in you. God poured out His Spirit onto those who believed and surrendered to His shaping process. The believers, including men and women, who believed the teaching of Jesus the Christ, anticipated the fulfillment of His promise, and had hope for a fully redeemed life, waited in the place where God told them to go. They were blessed in their obedience. In the simple act of gathering in obedience, they were blessed with power and a testimony through the Gospel to free not only Jews but the establishment of the church throughout all the Gentiles and into the world. The 120 were given the capacity as vessels of the King for his noble use and in just a short time they were increased to over 3,000.

If you walk in faith and obedience as Abraham, you too have the potential to give birth to dreamers and have the ability to produce children of faith. You can be as Noah who was found blameless among the people and chosen to be a remnant in the earth. Thousands of years ago, Noah took God's Word and through patience and obedience built what God told him to, did what God told him to, gathered what God told him to, and saved himself and provided a safe haven for the preservation of God's creation to which now we can witness today.

Have you surrendered your will to God's perfecting process? What would happen if you do not hesitate to do what God says do and go where He says to go? Have you decided to move forward and faithfully walk in the faith and integrity of the Word to fulfill your call to righteousness under the direction and partnership of the Holy Spirit and the men and women of God, the Father has sent you?

Move forward, Wonderful One, all things are possible in God. The endless possibility of a life in Christ and Christ in you awaits.

Lord God,

You are faithful to Your Word. I am grateful to have You on my side. I shall never be afraid of what the world may think. Whenever You speak to me and make Your vision clear, I move according to Your will. Time and time again I have witnessed Your favor when believers obey Your commands. I have heard of Your mighty works from the beginning when You told Abraham to go and He stepped out on faith and went to a place about which he had no idea. Abraham, even as an old man, was given the promise and the capacity to be the father of all nations because he moved forward with the utmost faith in You. Give me the faith not only to believe all that you have promised but also the faith to receive all that You have for me.

Thank You for your Holy Spirit that empowers me to build in humble submission like Noah because I heard Your command. Let me proceed on the path You've laid out for me so that I may receive my purpose and be overcome with Your Holy Spirit like Mary as You increase in me and use me for Your glory. I am not ashamed to do what is right. I will gather in Your name and proclaim Your goodness to everyone I encounter. I will wait upon You to fulfill every aspect of Your plan for me. I will never be afraid to choose to seek Your will instead of man's.

Lord, when I sincerely purposed to live and obey You and You only, You've directed me and led me to a ministry to develop my gifts and help me to realize how valuable I am to You. When I said 'Yes' to Your free gift of salvation, the heavenly realm was opened up to me. The heavens opened up when I surrendered to You, Your Spirit descended upon me, and since then I have been in Your presence and long to constantly please You.

Heavenly Father, with each step I take in You, You provide everything that I need. Every time I say 'Yes' You provide more and more of what I need to glorify You. Your Holy Spirit burns within me to eliminate the undesirable aspects of who my flesh tries to be and makes room for more of You within me. It is Your power that transforms my impurities to holiness. This power cannot be bought and manufactured; it comes from You when I am repentant, obedient, and willing to receive. O Merciful Father, Your Spirit ignites my heart with a passionate desire to serve You as I serve Your people. Your Holy Spirit continues to increase my ability to pray with power, prophesy, experience dreams and visions, and encounter You through worship ever increasing my ability to minister Your Word and change the lives of others as You have changed me.

When I move forward in obedience and am in full awareness of my purpose as an imperfect, earthen vessel faithfully walking in Your will and the integrity of the Word which reminds me that I can do all things, I have the capability to receive Your call to righteousness under the direction and partnership of the Holy Spirit and the awesome men and women of God You have gifted to lead me on this journey toward perfection in pursuit of Your endless possibilities. In Jesus Name, Amen.

Danielle Osonduagwuike

CAPACITY: *Reaching the Point of Perfected Performance*

*C*apacity is reaching the Point of Perfected Performance. "I can do all things through him who strengthens me (Philippians 4:13). Two important truths you can learn from God's Word are these: you are what God says you are, and you can do what God says you can do.

God has placed a desire for himself in every person. He draws man to himself and facilitates man's search. Man is called to speak with God and be in communion with him. Historically, man's religious beliefs have been expressed in many diverse ways. These religious expressions show that man is a "religious being." "God made all peoples, so that they would search for him" according to Acts 17:26-27.

Many factors (ignorance, evil, greed, bad examples, teachings hostile to God's purpose and promise) lead man to reject his "sincere bond to God." Out of fear, man hides himself (Genesis 3:8-10). Graciously, God still calls man to seek him, and every person must search for God with his intellect, will and "a sincere heart." "You have made us for yourself, and our heart is restless until it rests in you" says St. Augustine.

When we love at perfected performance through capacity we realize in our pursuit of the mystery that it is God's will for each of us to be "perfected in love" (John 4:12,17,18). "Perfected" does not mean sinless; it means fully developed, mature, attaining expert competence. God created each of us to become uniquely and fully developed in our ability to love, or as Jesus puts it elsewhere, that we "love others in the same way that I love you"

(John.13:34; 15:12). One scholar looking at this says it this way, "It is shallow enough for babies to wade in—but deep enough for elephants to drown in" So here is a very simple but challenging question: "Are you more proficient at this than you were a year ago?" This is God's test for true spirituality, and the search of capacity.

No matter how much more wealthy, physically fit, career advanced, popular, comfortable, etc. I am—if I am not becoming a better lover of my spouse, children, neighbors, work-mates, friends, the poor, my enemies, members of the church etc., I am failing in the classroom of life! I lack the capacity for perfected performance. Conversely, no matter how unimpressive my gains may be in these others areas, if I have become a better lover I am succeeding in life! This much is simple and shallow enough for babies to attain. But when we ask: "How do I do this?" the pool deepens.

John's answer, woven throughout this passage, is two-fold. If I want to be perfected in love, which is perfected performance, I must develop/increase both my capacity to receive God's love, and I must develop/increase my capacity to give his love away to others. There is a dynamic relationship between these two aspects of being perfected in love. On the one hand, since God is the source of all true love, we must increase our capacity to receive God's love in order to be better able to give it away to others. This is the point of 1 John 4:19. But on the other hand, we need to give God's love away to others in order to increase our capacity to receive God's love. This is the point of 1 John 4:12.

It gets even deeper, because being perfected in the performance of love develops both sequentially and simultaneously. We tend to think sequentially about this: first I'll learn how to receive God's love, and then after I master this I'll learn to give his love away to others. And there is some basic truth to this. But there is a sense in which this is misleading, because what this passage teaches and what real life confirms in having the capacity for perfected performance: is that God is always multi-tasking in this area of capacity to being perfected in love—simultaneously initiating our development in both receiving and giving his love. Just because you have His love your capacity for perfected performance is still not realized until you are able to give the same to others.

John breaks this into two stages—initially allowing God to indwell you with his love, and then continually drawing upon God's love in order that God might love through you. In other words we in pursuing the mystery of perfected love allow God to indwell us with His love first (1 John 4:9-15). You must first have the capacity to love which only comes from God's indwelling presence. You can't give to others what you don't have in yourself. Before you can give God's love to others, you must be indwelt by God's love yourself. John explains how to do this in 4:9-15. It is super-simple, but many people skip over it.

If you want to be indwelt by God's love, you need to first understand how much God loves you (1 John 4:9,10). He loves you so much that he gave you the ultimate gift (he sent his Son) to pay the ultimate price (he laid down his life to pay for your sins)—even though he knew you were completely undeserving (not only didn't love God, but were a rebel and transgressor). This is the truest example of capacity for perfected performance. If you were the only human being who ever rebelled against God, he loves you so much that he would have sent Jesus to die for just for you. You may say, "This is too good to be true"—but it is true. You may say, "No one else has ever loved me this way"—but God does love you this way, and he wants to personally indwell you with his love.

How? If you want to be indwelt by God's love, you need to personally agree with God that Jesus is indeed your Savior (1 John 4:15). "Confess" here means literally "to say the same thing as"—to agree from the heart. To confess that Jesus is the Son of God is to tell God in your own words that you agree with him when he says that you need a Savior and that Jesus is that Savior. Some people do this by talking to God silently; others do this by talking to God aloud. Some people do this alone; others do it in the presence of others. Some people say this with their own words; others do this by praying a written prayer that says this. What matters is that you personally tell God that you agree with him that you need a Savior and that Jesus is your Savior and your Lord.

When you confess Jesus is your Savior, he sends his Spirit to indwell you so you can experience his perfected love (1 John 4:13). He becomes your loving heavenly Father and you become his beloved child—and his Spirit enables you to feel his love for you. This is why people who have recently received Christ are excited—they have experienced the greatest thing possible for human beings to experience—they know they are loved by God! They enter the mystery of perfected love.

Are you indwelt by God's love? Has God's Spirit indwelt your heart? Have you confessed to God that Jesus is your Savior? If not, why not?

The next level of capacity and reaching the point of perfected performance is to draw continually upon God's love (1 John 4:16-19). It's not enough to be indwelt by God's love. In order to develop the capacity for the perfected performance of loving others, you also have to continually draw upon the love of God that already indwells you. John explains how to do this in 1 John 4:16,17. Notice the two ways he says we do this.

"We know... the love God has for us." So clarity of our perspective offers us the capacity of understanding and appreciating God's love for us as it becomes ever-fresh and ever-increasing. God's love is like a fine diamond—a multi-faceted wonder of brilliance, depth and clarity. We should keep discovering new facets of God's love, as we pursue the mystery of perfection through perfected performance of love for God and one another and we should keep discovering greater depths of each facet as we draw continuously nearer to God. If I am honestly bored by the truth that God loves me (and to our shame we must admit that sometimes we are bored by this), and the challenges of loving others, when this happens this is an alarm for my spiritual life signaling the need to learn more about God's love.

The main way we grow in our knowledge of God's love is by prayerfully reflecting on what scripture says about God's love. Ask God to open the eyes of your heart to his love (Ephesians 3:17-19), and then read and mediate on scripture looking for what it teaches about God's love that through it you may reach the point of capacity and perfected performance. Look for how God loves you not only in the Psalms but also in the Epistles or letters of the New Testament. When passages speak to your heart, speak them back to God. Sing spiritual songs that focus on God's love. This will build your capacity to refresh your heart with God's love, and it will build a growing and deepening foundation of God's love for you.

"We... rely on the love God has for us." As you learn more about how God loves you, he also provides you with many personal and practical ways to rely on his love. And as you choose to rely on his love, your experience of his love will expand and your confidence in the mystery of his love and the capacity to perfect the performance of sharing it will increase. Here are some of these ways:

You can rely on God's love by choosing to draw near to him (especially when you feel unworthy) rather than avoid him. This is what John means in 1 John 4:18. We all tend to make our own performance the basis for our right to come into God's presence. God says we are never worthy to come into his presence or the mystery of His perfect love on the basis of what I have done for him, but we are always worthy to come into his presence on the basis of what Jesus has done for us. On His capacity for perfected love is our capacity revealed. My question is: When was the last time you did this?

You can rely on God's love by choosing to let his people love you (especially in your weakness and sin) rather than remaining aloof, self indulgent, superficial and self-sufficient. Sometimes drawing near to God is not enough. Sometimes he waits until you open up to his people and let them know about your sin and hurt and doubt—and then he comforts your heart through their love as you reach the point of perfected performance and the capacity to love back.

You can rely on God's love by choosing to thank God for his love (especially when you have painful circumstances) rather than grumbling, murmuring and always complaining about everything and everyone. Chronic grumbling and complaining (differentiate from expressing pain to God and others) signals unbelief in God's love. We can't wait until we feel thankful to give thanks. We have to take ourselves in hand and (starting wherever we can) name how God blessed us and personally thank him for these blessings. What's your complaining/thankfulness ratio been lately? Do you need to build your capacity in this area?

You can rely on God's love by choosing to give his love to others (especially when you feel needy & inadequate) rather than waiting until you feel fully loved or adequate. This may sound contradictory—but this is the dynamic relationship I was talking about earlier. When I withhold God's love from others, this shows that I don't trust him to love me—and my capacity to receive his love shrinks. This is why habitually selfish Christians are never excited about God's love. But when I choose to trust God's love for me by giving his love to others even when I feel empty, God's love refreshes my soul as it pours itself out through me—and my capacity to receive and appreciate God's love grows as I build my capacity for perfected performance of His mystery of perfected love.

Meditation . . .

COMMITMENT...to a Life Worth Dying For
To Christ and His Sincerely Empowered Church

But is now made manifest by the appearing of our Savior Jesus Christ, who hath abolished death, and hath brought life and immortality to light through the gospel: Whereunto I am appointed a preacher, and an apostle, and a teacher of the Gentiles. For the which cause I also suffer these things: nevertheless I am not ashamed: for I know whom I have believed, and am persuaded that he is able to keep that which I have committed unto him against that day. ***2 Timothy 1:10-12 KJV***

Think back to where you used to be. Where were you when you heard God's voice and finally surrendered to His call to salvation? Don't cringe...that was you—the lying, cheating, stealing, intoxicated, selfish unbeliever. Oh well, maybe you weren't that bad. Maybe you were just unfaithful or so judgmental of Christians that you talked yourself and others out of ever going or desiring to be in church.

Just like Paul you have a history of being used by the enemy to keep you and others from your destiny. But our God full of grace and mercy saved Paul from sin. Paul was knocked off his course to destruction and given the gift of a fully redeemed life in Christ. As he sits in his prison, Paul reflected on all he gave up. He gave up foolishness, doubt, and death and committed his life to serving the true and wise God who saved him and set him on course to his perfecting process. What an exchange- death and hopelessness for life and hopefulness.

Paul has forgotten what is behind him. He has committed his life to pressing toward the mark of the high calling. Paul is not working for fortune or fame but merely living and loving for God who saved him. His gratefulness and intimate relationship with Christ has led him to encourage others while he sits waiting in his prison. Paul cannot see those he is writing to but has faith that in their service they are united in spirit and he desires to urge Timothy and the other apostles to keep focused, keep moving, and go forth in their renewed life.

Paul's example as overseer and shepherd of God's flock shows that he pledged his life to God and vowed to do His will no matter what. Paul was clear about his reality as the least to be called out to serve God and have such revelation and insight into His mysteries. The Christian persecutor was persecuted for saving others with the same gospel truth that he denied in his past.

This reality humbled Paul and motivated him to endure hardships, isolation, and betrayal unto death. As Jesus did, so did Paul. He heard God's voice, took up his cross and followed Christ until the end of his life. Paul's journey from salvation to death was worth living. Empowered by the Holy Spirit and mature in his faith, Paul gave up his life to build in Jesus name. His witness was that of a life apprehended by God to fortify the gospel message with the Jews and build the church through the Gentile nation. Instead of being bitter and broken through his exile and in the face of reality of a martyr's death, Paul encouraged churches, carried out the great commission, and wrote letters to guide and provide instruction in Christ's doctrine. How many of us give up when someone at church looks at us wrong, we are not listened to, or we just plain don't like what's going on? How many people can you name just walk away when it gets hard and take their gift and newly resurrected selves and walk away from the church and God? What cause is greater than that of the Lord? Is that your witness?

Paul's commitment was to Christ and the edification of a sincerely empowered church and what God built in and through him was made to last and benefit all who believe until the end of the earth. What a commitment, God and his sincere servant until death do they part!

Dear God,

You are my rock and my salvation. You are my redeemer and have saved me from the darkest places in my life. Your forgiveness is matchless. I am grateful that You are not a man that would change His mind. From the very beginning, You have given purpose to my life. Thank You for patiently waiting for me. Thank You for entering into my life in a supernatural way. You knocked me off my own ideals, blinded me to the ways of the world, and deafened my ears to nothing else but Your Word. I am fully confident in the power of the blood of Jesus that called me from being hell-bound to holiness.

Faithful Master, I called You Lord and gave my life to You without full knowledge of Your wisdom. My first inclination was to lean on Your hope but in my persistent pursuit of Your wisdom and way, I humbly seek to reflect Your image and build Your kingdom. Prosperity in You is nothing that anyone could ever imagine. It is a mystery of peace and joy even in the times of adversity. It is loving and trusting You more even when the enemy pursues me.

I am encouraged because You have begun a good work in me and You have promised that You will not finish it until the day of Jesus Christ. I am not ashamed of the gospel. I proclaim it in my thoughts, words, and actions. My unwavering faith comes each time I hear the testimony of Your grace and see how you save others just like me.

I can do no divine work in and of myself. Without You, Lord, I am nothing. I commit all things to You. With You nothing is impossible for me.

You have left Your Word and faithful example which has instructed me to do all things in the exact same way that Jesus Christ does. I must nail my sin to the cross. Deny worldly ambition and persist in being the reflection of Your image You have created me to be. With You as my Guide and Master Instructor, I am destined to do great things. For such things, God, all you have required is a fully committed heart.

Heavenly Father, You love me unconditionally and continually show me what I must do in this earth. You said You will do more things in and through me that will fill hearts with wonder and astonishment. By the blood and will of Jesus, I have been given eternal life. I have confessed my vow and taken a stand with Him as a covenant partner. He predestined me to be a living testimony to His grace. Through me, He still raises the dead and gives them life.

I am entirely in the hands of Jesus and I shall never be condemned. I honor Jesus with my life. My ears have been opened to receive the Word of God with understanding and I have put my total trust and reliance on the power of my heavenly Father to fulfill it in my life.

Thank You for the new life You have created for me in You. I regret nothing. I won't look back to what's behind me. I move forward denying my will daily and commit fully to my life in Christ and His Sincerely Empowered Church--- a life worth dying for.

Danielle Osonduagwuike

COMMITMENT: Reaching the Point of Consistently Seeking Eternal Possibilities

Commitment is reaching the Point of Consistently Seeking Eternal Possibilities. "As obedient children, let yourselves be pulled into a way of life shaped by God's life, a life energetic and blazing with holiness. God said, "I am holy; you be holy" (1 Peter 1:13-16 The Message). One of the great dangers in studying behavior in the Christian life is the danger of forgetting that behavior is in essence the reflection of character. And in the case of the sincere Christian, it is the character of God that is being demonstrated, when the Holy Spirit enables the Christian to behave then Satan wants to move us to one of two extremes. Either he wants us to view our behavior as something we have no control over, or as something we, in our own energy must do to please God.

It seems that today, no matter where you go there are people, young and old alike who are uncommitted. They have the appearance of commitment. They talk the talk they just don't walk the walk. Their actions speak louder than their words telling of half-hearted conditional commitment. See if these sound familiar. "Lord, I'll come to church but only on Sunday Morning." "Lord, I'll come to church every time the doors are open but don't expect me to do outreach, to teach a class, or pray publicly." "Lord, I'll do anything for you as long as it doesn't cost me anything."

I know that I am being a little harsh maybe but I don't want to be a part of a group of people that has little or no wholehearted commitment to God's purpose and plan. I am at a place in my life where I am ready to see people, young and old alike sold out to God.

Well, just what is commitment? Commitment is following Jesus. Commitment demands a choice. Jesus wasted no time getting to the heart of commitment: Either the disciples would be committed to Him and deny their own desires or they would be determined to go their own ways and deny Him. The choice to commit is the same for all believers - either deny ourselves or deny Him; either go His way or we pursue our own way or that of the enemy.

Talk about Christ would be meaningless without the walk with Him the wisdom of a committed witness of our faith in Him. The disciples were to take up their crosses. Carrying the cross beam was a public declaration of Rome's authority. Jesus challenged them to put themselves voluntarily under God's authority instead, doing His will, His way, and making a commitment to pursuing His mystery of perfection. Commitment demands action; it cannot be divorced from responsibility. It extends beyond our relationship to our heavenly Father to other areas of our life as well.

Ruth's words of commitment to Naomi did not speak as loudly as did her actions. She left her family and homeland to return with Naomi to Bethlehem as a Moabite among Jewish people. Her actions of commitment spoke louder than just her talking about being committed, but she unlike her sister Orpah, in the end didn't leave Naomi to travel the road to Bethlehem alone Ruth stayed committed (Ruth 1;15-19).

Commitment definitely limits choices because it is exclusive. For example, in a commitment to marriage, God's plan is for one woman and one man to commit to each other exclusively and permanently. Commitment builds up faith and develops character. It is a spiritual discipline requiring time, work and determination. Is it really possible to have this kind of commitment? Well, come here Peter and Paul and bear witness to your commitment. How about the fact that Peter-died crucified upside down or how Paul who during His ministry was so committed to Christ that he was: -jailed, beaten, starved, stoned, ridiculed, run out of town, and eventually killed. He even stayed committed while serving Christ with a problem he couldn't get rid of, he called it a "thorn in his flesh."

Likewise, Joshua 24:14 says God at a gathering of the people instructs Israel to "fear the Lord, serve Him in sincerity and in truth." This instruction appears in a particular context. The people of Israel had spent 40 years wandering around in the wilderness, had thereafter crossed the River Jordan into the land of Canaan, and then fought with the Canaanites for possession of the land that was promised to them by God. After a number of years of struggle, the Promised Land was finally theirs; each Israelite now possessed his own parcel of land in Canaan. So it is that, at the end of the meeting described here, "Joshua let the people depart, each to his own inheritance" (vs. 28). In a word, the promise which God had made to Abraham about His commitment to giving the land of Canaan to his descendants has been fulfilled; Israel was securely settled in the Promised Land.

That in turn means that now Israel's life as God's covenant people may begin in earnest. Israel had come to a certain maturity;

their period of youthful training in the wilderness was over. Now that they're settled, it was God's holy wish that each of His children move forward in pursuit of the mystery of perfection as seen in the commitment to acting responsibly and independently as a child of God. So it was that God did not appoint a successor to the aged Joshua; from now on the Lord expected His people to live in agreement with their responsibilities as bearers of the mystery of perfection-of-all-believers. Yes, the people of Israel still had elders and heads and judges and officers (vs. 1), but the people, under their leadership, should now themselves work with God's revelation as revealed to them over the years past; no longer would they have a central leadership (seen in the leadership of Moses and then Joshua) to tell them how to live and act in the various situations in which they'd find themselves. They themselves would have to make a commitment to pursuing the mystery of perfection as believers through their own intimate and personal relationship with God.

As the people stood on the threshold of this new era-of-greater-personal-responsibility, there was one matter which God wished Joshua yet to discuss with Israel before he died. And that is the matter of impressing upon the people the need for choosing whether or not they shall serve the Lord wholeheartedly, the need for commitment to the Lord. That's the reason why Joshua summoned Israel together here in Joshua chapter 24.

With all Israel gathered before him in Shechem, then, Joshua laid before the people the command of God to "fear the Lord, and serve Him...." The question that immediately comes to mind is this: why should Israel bother to serve this God as they continue moving forward?

The reason is found in Joshua's choice of name for God in our text. Joshua makes a point of telling Israel to "fear the LORD." We realize that the word LORD with capital letters is the translation of God's covenant name Yahweh. That name in turn catches the notion of God's commitment to faithfulness, the notion that God is-Who-He-says-He-is and nothing will prevent God from doing as He'd said. Joshua spells that out in the first 13 verses of the chapter.

The witness to *Commitment* as reaching the Point of Consistently Seeking Eternal Possibilities and is seen as Joshua made mention of the fact that Israel's fathers had once lived in Ur of the Chaldeans, and there served strange gods. Despite being heathens, however, the Lord "took your father Abraham" (vs. 3) and promised him the land of Canaan. God made a commitment to consistently seek eternal possibilities for them even when they were heathens.

It was not that Abraham deserved this promise from God; the fact that he served other gods made him as damnable before God as any other person. Yet God took him, promised him a bright future - why? Simply because it pleased God to do so; here was God's mercy: His Commitment.

Further, this God gave to Abraham (in his old age) a child, Isaac. To Isaac in turn were given the two boys Jacob and Esau. Of those two covenant children, God loved the one, but hated the other. He chose to make a commitment to Jacob, but rejected Esau: this is what we know as election/reprobation. It wasn't that Jacob deserved this election more than Esau. Yet God chose him, why?

Simply because God was committed to doing so; He continues to show love for the unworthy: His Commitment.

Israel went to Egypt and spent some 400 years there. Yet God did not forget this people; He remembered His covenant commitment and gave them deliverance in a wonderful way through the hand of Moses and Aaron. Was it deserved? Certainly not; Israel in Egypt was far from pious, far from committed, far from faithful. Yet, God granted deliverance: His Commitment.

For forty years Israel traveled through the wilderness, grumbling as they went. Yet when Balak sought Balaam's assistance to curse Israel, God rose up in defense of this people and turned the intended curse into a blessing. Was it deserved? Again, the answer is no! Yet, God delivered Israel from the curse, caused the blessing, because God was pleased to love this unworthy people: His Commitment.

Let's look a little deeper into this story of commitment that shows us what can happen when we reach the point of consistently seeking eternal possibilities. Frightened by the fall of the lands of the Amorites and Bashan, the kings of Moab and Midian, the Israelites foes for many generations, united for the purpose of a common attack upon the children of Israel. Balak, the newly elected king of Moab, had been put in charge of the plans to hold back Israel and attempt to keep them from the land. Thinking of the surprising victories of the outnumbered troops of the Jewish people, Balak came to the conclusion that these victories could only be attributed to some form of magic and not the eternal possibilities of their God. He believed that the only way to destroy the victorious Jews was to outdo them in magic by a spell stronger than theirs.

Balak, therefore, sent messengers to Balaam, the greatest magician of those days, asking him to come to Moab to curse the people of Israel who were threatening to overrun their lands. Balaam knew that he could not do anything against God's will, and he so informed king Balak, even though his personal hatred of the Jews made him only too willing to follow the call.

However, king Balak was persistent. He sent an imposing delegation of princes and nobles and promised Balaam more gold and silver. Balaam received the delegation with the respect due to their rank. Regretfully, he told them that even if king Balak gave him a full house of gold and silver, he could not go against God's command. He asked them, however, to stay overnight, because only at night was he privileged to receive Divine inspiration. During that night, Balaam had a vision in which he was informed that he might go with Balak's men, but that he was not to say anything save the words that God Himself would put into his mouth.

Balaam rose early in the morning, saddled his ass, and went with the princes of Moab. But God was angry at Balaam's eagerness to do harm to the Jewish people, and He sent an angel to hinder his way, the ass saw the angel of God with a drawn sword, and she tried to evade him by stepping off the path. Balaam, who did not perceive the angel, got angry and hit the ass in order to guide her back to the path.

A little while later, the angel with the drawn sword blocked the way on a narrow vineyard path, fenced by walls on either side. Trying to avoid the angel, the ass pressed herself close to the wall, thereby hurting Balaam's foot. Again Balaam hit the ass. Now the angel placed himself squarely across the path where there was no chance of avoiding him, so this time the ass lay down, refusing to move forward.

Now Balaam was in such a rage that he savagely hit the ass with his staff for the third time. At this moment, God gave the ass the ability to speak. The ass asked the astonished Balaam why he had beaten her these three times. Her master, stupefied, though still in a rage, replied that he would have killed her, had he only had a sword handy. Yet while Balaam spoke, God opened his eyes to see the eternal possibilities of his own demise, and he saw the angel with the sword drawn in his hand. At this Balaam bowed in reverence.

The Angel told Balaam that it was he who had blocked the way, and that Balaam had done an injustice to the ass. Balaam excused himself, saying that he had not known that God wanted to prevent his trip, and that he was ready to return. But the angel replied that he should continue his journey, remembering to say only that which God would tell him.

When king Balak heard of Balaam's arrival, he went out to meet him and took the prophet up to the heights sacred to the Moabite god Baal. There they built seven altars, upon each of which they sacrificed an ox and a ram. Then Balaam went alone to a solitary place, hoping to receive the word of the Lord. When he returned to the king, he had beheld a vision, and he felt inspired. He stood near his burnt-offering before king Balak and the princes of Moab, and urged by an irresistible impulse, he broke forth into blessings. "How can I curse whom God has not cursed?" Balaam (Numbers 23:8) exclaimed. He went on to praise the marvelous people, the children of Israel which will never lose its identity among the nations of the world, and concluded with the words (Numbers 23:10): "May my soul die the death of the upright and let my end be like his!" Hearing Balaam's divinely inspired praise of Israel, king Balak became angry at Balaam for blessing his enemies instead of cursing them. Balaam replied that he could say only what God put in his mouth.

Again king Balak prepared sacrifices, and Balaam waited for an inspiration to curse the Jewish people. However, God put praise and blessings into his mouth. "God is not a man that He should lie, nor is He a mortal that He should relent. Would He say and not do, speak and not fulfill? I have received [an instruction] to bless, and He has blessed, and I cannot retract it. He does not look at evil in Jacob, and has seen no perversity in Israel; the Lord, his God, is with him..." Again, we see God's Commitment to those He chooses to move into the mystery of His perfection to reach the point of consistently seeking eternal possibilities instead of the limited perspectives of this world.

The inhabitants of the Promised Land were, in military terms, a people far superior to the wilderness wandering Israelites. Yet, God gave the lands of these peoples to the Israelites; Canaan became their inheritance, their Promised Land. And that too was categorically not because Israel was more worthy than any other nation. Yet God gave them this land of abundance -why? Again, simply because of His own good pleasure; He loved them, chose them, delivered them, and blessed them, all because He had promised in the covenant to do so. He was committed. You see, beloved, He is the Lord. Who is Who He says He is. He is eternal possibilities.

And there, you have the reason why Israel should serve this God. That history over the years pointed out that the Lord was so much more than the god that Abram used to serve in Ur, was so much more than the gods of Egypt, more than the god of Balak, more than the gods of the Canaanites and the Amorites and the Perizzites and the Hivites. Both in terms of sheer strength, as well as it terms of commitment, mercy and love, Israel's God was far superior to the gods of the nations. So it follows: this is the God whom Israel is to serve. As Joshua says in our text, "Now therefore, fear the Lord, and serve Him...; put away the gods which your fathers served on the other side of the River and in Egypt. Serve the Lord!" And we say: Yes, of course this is the God Israel is to serve; in light of what He's done, that's only obvious.

But consider now ourselves. You know that those physical acts which God did for Israel are also pictures of what God has done for us today. God has 'taken' us too and made His covenant commitment with us. He also 'chose' us, worked faith; called or elected us. He gave us 'deliverance', for He sent His Son and through His commitment seen the historical events of; Christmas (or His birth), Good Friday, Easter, Pentecost –He obtained our redemption. And no, we know that we are not yet fully in the Promised Land, for the New Jerusalem has not yet come down from heaven. But we have already the beginning; we are children of God, and His Holy Spirit dwells within us as a guarantee that the remainder of our inheritance is sure to come. Because God has been faithful in His commitment to us, God has also given us a place in this beautiful corner of His creation, has given us churches and schools, homes and so much more than we deserve. Already we've received so much, and when Christ comes back we're going to receive more still.

So we understand that the command of our text is true for us today even more than it was for Israel. Given all that God has given to us and done for us, "what can we render unto God for all His many benefits,"(Psalm 116:12). We too are to "fear the Lord, and [commit to] serve Him." We realize that, and so we say yes, we certainly want to serve the God who has given us so much; of course we do. We want to fear the Lord, and we don't mean that we want to be filled with fright or anxiety or dread of God; instead, we want to stand in awe of God's eternal possibilities and the mystery of His perfection, to be filled with reverence for our God who has through His committed use of power and mercy has blessed unworthy sinners like us. Yes, we're thankful that God has given us so much, and so we want to pursue the mystery of perfection by serving Him with all our heart and soul. We share Israel's enthusiasm when they reached the point of Commitment and thus Consistently Seeking Eternal Possibilities: "We also will serve the Lord, for He is our God."

Meditation . . .

*CONFIDENCE---In the Embrace of God's Ultimate Purpose for Our Lives

> *But ye are a chosen generation, a royal priesthood, an holy nation, a peculiar people; that ye should shew forth the praises of him who hath called you out of darkness into his marvelous light; which in time past were not people, but are now the people of God; which had not obtained mercy, but now have obtained mercy. Dearly beloved, I beseech you as strangers and pilgrims, abstain from fleshly lusts, which wage war against the soul; Having your conversation honest among the Gentiles that, whereas they speak against you as evil-doers, that may be good works, which they shall behold, glorify God in the day of visitation.* **1 Peter 2:9-12 KJV**

God's plan was for men and women to reign in the earth. Even after the fall, the new start with Noah, and the disappointment in Moses leadership, our forgiving God persisted with his plan of redemption. God called the people of Israel out of bondage and promised them a land where they would prosper. From among them He called out the Levites and ordained them to a life of service. A king, Saul, was then chosen by the people. Saul's reign ended when God once again stepped in to elevate a man after his own heart, David. God called out this young man from among those who others thought could be king. God looked at the heart and not the outer appearance. He claimed David and no one could deny his call.

David with his passion for God led His people with the tenderness of a shepherd and the unconditional love of the father.

The chosen one, David, was the gentle shepherd tending to sheep who could only live according to how he led them. If he did not lead them to the pasture to eat, they would starve. If David was not bold enough to step in and make a sacrifice to fight predators such as bears and lion, they would die. If he did not worship and listen to the voice of God as he ran through every challenge, triumph, move and mistake, he would have without strength.

The Lord established the kingdom structure in the earth led by a king who ministered to his people, fought like a champion warrior, worshiped in spirit and truth, and praised God through every battle. He was a royal priest.

Through King David, we have an example of how we are to function in our kingship as given here on earth. We are to have power and authority to take the world by force and restore it with patience, led by the Spirit, and by the instruction found in the Holy Scriptures.

Our part is to keep doing, keep moving, and keep pursuing in His name. Believe the Word not the world like King David. You are chosen.

Chosen... to be elected, selected, special, preferred. Wow! What an identity! There is security in knowing you are chosen out of millions of people in the world. God chose you to be His people to care for, to love, to bless and live a life with Him for all eternity.

Individually you have been called out and saved by grace to be a disciple in the body of Christ. God came to you and pulled you out of the darkness and bondage of sin into His marvelous light, raised you up and sealed You with the covenant blood of His Son Jesus the Christ. You received a new identity with the Spirit of the Lord as an heir, God's child.

The Word states if we keep the commands of the Lord and walk in His ways, God will establish you as a holy people. Corporately, we make up the body of Christ and are called to be a holy people--- one rooted and built up on the foundation of God's truth. The truth is that He carried us on eagles' wings and brought us to Himself. (Ex. 19:4) As God's treasured possessions, we belong to Him as long as we keep His command.

We must move forward in the confidence of and security in our identity as predestined. We must stay close, stay focused, and sure of whom we serve. Find security in our God-given identity. It's our destiny as God's chosen to rule, reign, and have authority in the earth.

With the security in knowing you are a child of God, how can a bad report, trying situation, or someone's words keep you down? Why do we settle for so much less than God's best. Any and everything kicks us down when God has already placed everything under our feet. Do you truly believe the Word?

Have you embraced God's purpose for your life? Are you excited about your forward movement through the mysteries of God's perfection?

Heavenly Father,

I Thank You that Your Word is faithful and true. You have chosen me to be your child through the sanctifying work of the Holy Spirit, the receiving of Jesus as my Lord and Savior, and the sacrifice of His blood on my behalf. Father, I repent for fighting battles for earthly status and earthly gain. It is Your Spirit that makes me rich. It is Your grace that has lifted me. God, Your unmerited favor, supernatural ability, bountiful blessings, and endless peace are mine to claim in abundance!

I Praise You God! Your great mercies toward me have given me a new birth and a living hope through the resurrection of Jesus. I am an heir to what can never expire or fade. My inheritance is secured for me in heaven right now.

Through faith, I am sure of what I hope for and certain of what I do not see. Through the confidence of my faith, I am shielded by God's power until the coming of the salvation that is to be revealed in the last day. In that day, all aspects of the curse will be removed and I will no longer have to fight to maintain what is mine as Your child.

Until then, I must fight. I must persevere through many griefs and trials which strengthen my faith because eternity awaits me. When I am tested through battles, insecurities, and the taunting of my flesh, I will not be tossed by every wave. I will trust You. When I don't know what to do, I will seek Your face and be guided by Your Word of truth. Like David, I will embrace my anointing and use the tools of my faith to stand against the enemy and declare to the nations who I am and who You are to me. I will have no fear, for You O God are my confidence. You shall preserve me in time of danger and keep my foot from being tripped up along the way. Fires and the pressures of this world will show and prove that my faith is genuine. My faith is precious and a greater commodity than gold.

My faith will endure and produce the fruit of the Spirit that dwells in me. It will result in praise, glory, and honor of You, my Father. Those who see me will know You are real through my testimony of your goodness and grace. I have not seen Jesus, but am a beneficiary of His mighty works and the receiver of the greatest gift of salvation. I love You Jesus. I believe in You in that You now sit at the right hand of our Father interceding for me as I walk faithful to Your Word each day of my life.

I Praise You, O God as I embrace Your purpose for my life---as Your child, Your chosen one. I receive my identity and am confident in my position in the royal priesthood in that when I present my body as a living sacrifice and gather together with other believers in Your name, we as the called out body praise You and declare Your promises to live life in abundance as we glorify and re-present Your image in the earth.

In Jesus' Holy and Matchless Name, Amen.

Danielle Osonduagwuike

CONSCIOUSNESS: Reaching the Point of Purposeful Confidence in the Divine Plan

Consciousness is reaching the Point of Purposeful Confidence in the Divine Plan. "This is the confidence we have in approaching God: that if we ask anything according to his will, he hears us" (I John 5:14).

The apostle John--who wrote the book of 1 John--was the only one of Jesus Christ's original apostles to not be murdered by the Roman government. Not that they didn't try! But John was an old man who didn't die easily. Eventually the Roman government banished John to an Island called Patmos. John was an eyewitness of Jesus Christ, one of the first of Jesus' followers, and in fact the youngest at the time, and he wrote five books in our New Testament: The gospel according to John (the fourth book of the New Testament), three letters--1st, 2nd, and 3rd John, and then finally the book of Revelation, the last book of the Bible. Before being banished to the Island of Patmos by the Roman Government, John served for many years as an overseer or bishop/apostle for all the churches in ancient Asia Minor.

Asia Minor is located in modern day Turkey, and there John lived as a kind of spiritual mentor-the last living apostolic witness to Christ's life, death and the incarnational embrace of His resurrection--so he kept himself busy helping the Christians in Asia Minor develop into fully devoted followers of the mystery of Jesus' ministry. John most likely wrote his Gospel for use among these churches in Asia Minor, to give them an accurate account of the life, death, burial and resurrection of Jesus Christ. He made them conscious of The Mystery of Perfection by leading them to a Purposeful Commitment to the Divine Plan.

Soon the Christians in Asia Minor became bitterly divided between those who held to this purposeful commitment about the mystery of Jesus and God's divine plan; and those who believed new and novel ideas about Jesus Christ. The fight was between religion and relationship; knowing about God and intimacy with God through the mystery of pursuing the Christ-life or the Divine Plan.

So John wrote his first letter in order to correct these misunderstandings about Jesus Christ and the Christian life in the face of this terrible division that was destroying the churches and causing Christians to take dangerous detours in their spiritual journey. You see, the Christians in Asia Minor had reached a major fork in the road in their spiritual journey, and the pursuit of the mystery of perfection with John as the last remaining living apostle calling for them to follow the divine plan of Jesus and with false teachers enticing the church to depart from this path to follow their new contemporary ideas of the times.

Eventually this painful split would deeply wound the churches in Asia Minor, causing terrible division, and leading many away from the pursuit of the mystery of perfection to follow a different plan and a false religion that later became known as Gnosticism. Ancient Gnosticism is really quite similar to what you and I know of today as the New Age Movement of anything goes and not the perfected-ness of following Christ and His divine plan.

John is writing this letter as a roadmap to help the confused and troubled Christians in Asia Minor navigate these unexpected twists and turns in the pursuit of the mystery of perfection, in Christ and to help them stay focused on the truth of Jesus and His divine plan and not be led astray down a different path. Shortly after writing this letter John was banished to Patmos, where he wrote the book of Revelation, and then he eventually died and was buried back in Asia Minor.

So one of John's reasons for writing his letter was to re-ignite joy in this spiritual journey in pursuit of the mystery of perfect and restore confidence in the divine plan. But not only do we need joy in the pursuit we need the right foundation for our journey, and we also need the right companions. John is sharing his experiences as an eyewitness so we can enter into fellowship with the clarity, capacity, commitment and consciousness of the apostles who represent the practical reflection of the mystery of perfection by their faith in the divine plan.

What we mean here is found in the word "fellowship" which is a problem for many believers today. We just want to come to church, hear what the sermon has to say about our personal situations and how this may be an answer to our individual prayers. When the truth is that the Greek word for fellowship in this idea is "koinonia," and it actually means a close relationship of sharing with other people. It can be described as the "setting aside of individual and private interest and desires and the joining in with others for common purposes. So John is sharing with us the mystery of perfection here though he himself is exiled to an island, he writes to perfect the consciousness of the saints for the work of the ministry and the pursuit of the mystery of perfection in living for Christ and sharing this Christ-life together.

This is reaching the point of "mutual sharing," whether it's sharing our lives, our hearts, our possessions, our tears, our struggles, our challenges, our frustrations or our blessings in conscious commitment to the divine plan. It is mutual, interconnected creating a sense of synergy and dependent consciousness to the sharing of life together. Reaching the point of conscious biblical fellowship is a relationship of both give and take with other followers of Jesus Christ in pursuit of the mystery of perfection. One of the primary purposes for the sincere Church is to provide a place for this experience of shared mutual fellowship with other Christians to occur.

In the letter of I John we learn that true fellowship is based on a common fellowship with God and God's Son Jesus Christ. In I John 1:4 we also learn of John's desire that there be joy in this spiritual pursuit of the mystery of perfection, that this joy might be fulfilling having confidence in the divine plan. Here we find the necessity of having the right companions in our spiritual pursuit of the mystery of perfection. Our pursuit is joyful when shared with others committed to the mystery of the perfection of our faith and fulfillment of the divine plan.

I Timothy states; "They must be committed to the mystery of the faith now revealed and must live with a clear conscience." The word "conscience" derives from Middle English, from Old French, and from the Latin "conscientia." It refers to the sense or consciousness of the moral goodness or blamelessness of one's own conduct, intentions, or character together with a feeling of obligation to do right or be good.

Secondly, it is the process, power, or principle connected to good acts. The conscience is the little voice God has given us in our heart (or head) to determine, based on what we know or have studied about the facts of a given situation, what is right and what is wrong. The conscience is moral consciousness and awareness. It is prompted based on its education and sensitivity (Acts 23: 1, 26: 9-14, I Timothy 1:13; Acts 24: 16). Conscience is viewed as a kind of microscope; keeping it clear or good means ensuring that it is not destroyed by circumstances.

The mystery of our faith or in other words the mystery of perfection or godliness is shown here as the richness in our worship as we confidently acknowledge the divine plan; keeping it clear that Jesus Christ is our Lord and Savior. Looking at the importance of the conscience I Timothy 1:5 says, "Now the end of the commandment is love out of a pure heart, and of a good conscience, and a sincere faith" (I Timothy 1: 5). The *utility of the conscience* can be seen when Paul says in Romans, "I say the truth in Christ, I lie not, my conscience also bearing me witness in the Holy Spirit" (Romans 9: 1).

The *appeal of the conscience* can be seen with this, "Therefore, since we know what it means to fear the Lord, we try to persuade people. We ourselves are perfectly known to God. I hope we are also really known to your consciences." (2 Corinthians 5:11). A *good conscious* is possible if we hold on to the mystery of perfection of our faith and commitment to the divine plan, "Holding the mystery of the faith in a pure conscience" (I Timothy 3: 9).

Likewise, *a dysfunctional conscience* is seen when Paul writes to Timothy, "Speaking lies in hypocrisy; having their conscience seared with a hot iron" (I Timothy 4: 2). God warns against an *evil conscience* as seen when the writer of Hebrews offers, "Let us draw near with a true heart in full assurance of faith, having our hearts sprinkled from an evil conscience...." (Hebrews 10: 22)

A good conscience then is the result of acting upon what God has said. The primary goal of God's perfect plan is to demonstrate the glory of God. A secondary goal is to accomplish the good of those who love God: "And we know that God causes all things to work together for good to those who love God, to those who are called according to His purpose" (Romans 8:28).

The ultimate good is that which manifests the perfection of God's glory. For the Christian, "good" includes the blessing of all those who are the called in Jesus Christ. The promised blessings of the Bible are the good which God has purposed and promised and guides our pursuit of the mystery of perfection. The Christian life should be lived out in the light of the superiority of God's promised blessings in comparison to the "blessings" an ungodly world holds out to us (Hebrews 11:24-26)

All of us are not called like Paul to be apostles, but each of us does have a God-given ministry as part of God's divine plan. We can share the gospel, suffer for Christ and fulfill the mystery of the ministry God has given us. We can commit to striving in prayer for God's people and encourage one another to maturity or perfection. As we grow in grace and in knowledge as Christians pursuing the mysteries of perfection we progress in preparation, partnership and purpose to live the Christ-life which is the divine plan and as such we can more easily defeat the enemy and not be led astray.

If our spiritual roots are deep in Christ - through clarity, capacity, commitment, and consciousness - than we will not desire any other soil. If Christ is our sure foundation, we have no need to move any direction but forward by grace and knowledge of Him as our Lord and Savior to His glory. Pursuing this mystery of perfection as a grounded, growing, grateful, believer we will not be led astray.

As we pursue the mystery of perfection we draw on Christ's fullness or perfection, which is the very fullness of God Himself. As we draw near, we are made complete (perfect) with all the fullness of life and power that comes from God (Ephesians 3:19). Thus we reach the point of **Purposeful Confidence in the Divine Plan** as we move ever forward into the mystery of perfection living the Christ-life.

Sanctified Conversation

Sanctified is to be set apart as sacred

Conversation is an interchanging of thoughts

So what is an interchanging of sacred and set apart thoughts?

This is prayer

The best type of communication

Where one may speak their mind until empty,

speak gratitude, speak of personal necessities,

and ask forgiveness of all seen and unseen iniquities

God listens to these

and if you're in the right place spiritually

not only does he listen

but respond

Speak, listen, respond, and listen

That's all there is to it

A sanctified conversation

___Zaina Goggins

2

PASSIONATELY PURSUING THE MYSTERY

The motivation for ministry service must be drawn from a slavish commitment to the mystery of the cause of Christ and the building of His kingdom.

Before you can pour a foundation, you first have to dig one. The truth of digging a foundation is that one must go down beneath the surface so that the foundation will be strong. This is why so many of us are suffering it is because our roots or foundation is not deep enough to withstand the life we are attempting to live. In order to really see the depth of what God is telling us in Scripture one has to first go beyond the surface of the text. Passion for Christ cannot be based entirely on what we get all the time as so many preach today but on what we give totally in righteousness.

> *"And there is no one who calls on Your name, who stirs himself up to take hold of You; for You have hidden Your face from us, and have consumed us because of our iniquities."* **(Isaiah 64:7, NKJV).** "

> *"With my soul I have desired You in the night, yes by my spirit within me I will seek You early; for when Your judgments are in the earth, the inhabitants of the world will learn righteousness."* **(Isaiah 26:9, NKJV).**

Passion is a motivator that continuously beckons us to move forward even in the face of opposition, struggle or setback.

Passion for God is borne out of a deep desire to have a more intimate and personal relationship with His Son Jesus. This passion produces a clarity, capacity, commitment and consciousness of the possibilities available in Him and convinces us by the pursuit of the mystery of His love that He is the only hope for us living in a sin sick and dying world. Passion requires that we dig deeper for the hidden truths beneath the surface of our superficial relationship with His grace and knowledge.

The truth is there are little treasures hidden beneath the surface level of your biblical text. There are things that God has hidden beneath the surface of the biblical text, that if we pursue the mystery of perfection, not being perfect, but by allowing ourselves to be perfected (through the foundation of clarity, capacity, commitment and consciousness) in our search for the concealed mysteries of God's truth, they will be revealed to us as a reward for our efforts.

Mark 4:22 says, "For there is nothing hidden which will not be revealed, nor has anything been kept secret but that it should come to light." When Jesus spoke these words He was speaking of the "Parable of the Sower." He was talking about a seed and how things had been hidden from people on purpose. So here in Mark 4 He begins to talk about the mysteries or the hidden things of God; things that God has hidden or concealed of His perfection or perfect work of redemption. But everything that God has concealed He will make known and He is going to reveal it.

So in Proverbs 25:2 it says, "It is the glory of God to conceal a matter, but the glory of kings is to search (pursue) out a matter." So the truth of the matter is that God does in fact conceal things.

There are things that are a mystery or are concealed from us by God. It is actually His glory to conceal things. The text says it is to the benefit of kings to pursue these things, hidden by God for His glory. He has concealed the mystery of perfection for us to pursue with focused clarity and passionate commitment.

In Amos 3:7, we discover, "Surely the Lord God does nothing, unless He reveals His secret (mystery of perfection) to His servants the prophets." So clearly we see that God surely has secrets or mysteries, and before these mysteries become made manifest or perfected, what God does is alert His people to what is His perfect plan although hidden and now about to be revealed. God's mystery of perfection or His secrets have been kept for a time but as that time approaches God reveals the mystery of His perfection to His people. Because you see, God wants us to know what He is doing in the earth and as we pursue His mystery of perfection may serve our perfect purpose and discover the true desires of our heart hidden just beneath the surface. It you truly love the Lord your passion will burn for the deeper things of life hidden in Him.

Unfortunately, there are far too many believers who think that God doesn't have anything He needs to conceal. In fact they say everything has already been revealed. We have all heard the saying that the Old Testament is the New Testament concealed, and the New Testament is just the Old Testament revealed; meaning that everything in the Old Testament that was hidden through Jesus Christ has been revealed. This ends up being like so many of our earthly relationships, where we stop searching for the things that help us grow more passionately committed to one another. Like Christian couch potatoes, we just sit and come to church, and maybe read the bible without much passion for life, love or the pursuit of a richer relationship with Christ and each other lying just beyond our limited reach, understanding and perspectives.

Though this is the Truth there are still things yet to be revealed to us, hidden for a time when God himself will reveal them. Who can read the Book of Revelation and say they understand all the mysteries contained therein. In fact the word for Revelation in the Greek is "Apokalupsis" which means "unveiling, or take off the cover." To unveil something means that something is hidden and the lid is being uncovered or taken off to reveal what has heretofore been a mystery.

So pursuing the mystery of perfection is not to presuppose that we understand everything there is to know about what God Himself has made perfect and concealed from us. There are people then, we must understand who have pursued religion and there are those who are in pursuit of an intimate and personal relationship. Religious people don't embrace the idea that we don't know it all and that there is so much more God has perfected, promised and planned to be revealed to those who would pursue passionately an intimate and personal relationship with Him.

So those who pursue the mystery of God's perfect plan, because they want to know Him and desire a relationship with Him understand that in any intimate relationship that as you pursue the benefits of seeking to know more about that person, more that is concealed will become revealed to you over time. Just ask your spouse how much more they know now that they've been with you awhile than they knew when first you begin the relationship.

We find as we seek a sincere relationship that through clarity, capacity, commitment and consciousness what you were attracted to initially is not what you are attracted to as you grow in grace and knowledge. You soon discover that you're passionate about things as you grow in the relationship that you hadn't even considered when you first started pursuing the relationship initially. You find that there are things at the depth that you happened to not even be aware of when just looking at the surface and only come out having experienced the relationship more intimately.

So if we pursue the life of faith as if we know everything and there is nothing else to learn, or is hidden from us in the Scriptures, then we will be confined by this religious attitude and will not pursue at a deeper level the things God has hidden of His mystery of perfection. When our desire is to establish an intimate and personal relationship with our Heavenly Father, through His Son, Jesus Christ, then as we grow in grace and in knowledge of Him and draw closer then the mystery or hidden, things will begin to be revealed.

"It is the glory of God to conceal a matter, but the glory of kings is to search (pursue) out a matter."(Proverbs 25:2). The key word here is to search out, which means to dig from the depths like a treasure hunt. When kings leave a treasure they leave it for their heirs. He leaves His treasure to people who will appreciate and be grateful for what he is leaving them. The king doesn't leave his treasure for just any one. Someone who might misappropriate his treasure and use it in ways he would not want it used. He doesn't leave the treasures of the kingdom to those that would dishonor it. So he doesn't leave his treasure laying around on the surface. He buries his treasure to hide it or conceal it for his heirs.

This is what we see in the Pyramids and sacred artifacts of Egypt, the treasure of the dynasties of African Kings called Pharaohs (not the ones we see in movies or have through ignorance been expressed in church) who concealed their treasures, intellectual, material, and spiritual treasures for those generations of future Kings stolen from Africa, only to be re-presented to the world and called negroes, colored folk, blacks, Afro- Americans, or African Americans to pursue and dig deeper in their desire to know and grow in the soil of their rich heritage. This will require that the King make them a map that leads them to this treasure.

THE RERUDJI CONCEPT:
Putting the Truth Back in the Church!

In the 1994, while working for the State of Iowa in Criminal and Juvenile Justice planning, I created a cultural development model "The Rerudj Concept" using various cultural elements consisting of African American psycho-social cultural theory to build a bridge between the understanding of present African American cultural particularities, and the historical, social, spiritual and political implications of not knowing the plethora of challenges facing African American families and communities in the 21st century.

The Rerudj Concept presented a matrix and minimum set of cultural values, ideas, analysis and culturally appropriate development strategies by which the culturally particular experiences of people of African descent, now called by many names, can be shared, understood and examined, even ultimately as I discovered by digging, the spiritually mystery of our cultural perfection as revealed through the glory of Jesus' death, burial and incarnational embrace through His resurrection. I soon learned that the glory of this was only to be revealed to me through the passionate pursuit of the mystery of perfection with clarity, capacity, commitment and consciousness. It soon became clear that although the message of the gospel never changes, the methods sometimes have to. With a more passionately focused, innovative, and creative method one could rediscover the hidden passion for the Truth lost, stolen or strayed from the moorings of reality.

What was once hidden, by the brutal history of struggle, system of intellectual incarceration, spiritual neglect and just plain destruction of the heritage and inheritance of a people and the hindrance of the manipulation of their story and possibilities through ignorance, could be overcome by passionately seeking to know Christ and His purpose for our lives through grace and knowledge.

The concepts and theories revealed by this passionate pursuit are a product of tradition and reason, of history and a response to current social/spiritual needs. The Rerudj Concept uses a critique and corrective approach to understanding African American social, familial, and community ideas, behaviors and practices. As a result of this analysis and critique the model than offered a specific set of culturally appropriate developmental ideas which construct a culturally appropriate problem solving matrix. I discovered a love for Christ, culture and community as a result.

The Rerudj Concept: *is adapted from an Ancient Kemetic (Egpytian) philosophy*

Restore and raise up that which is in ruin
Repair that which is damaged
Heal that which is wounded
Repair that which is separated
Replenish that which is lacking
Make strong that which is weak
Make flourish that which is fragile and
Underdeveloped and needs to flourish

Son of man, prophesy against the shepherds of Israel...Woe be to the shepherds of Israel that do feed themselves! Should not the shepherds feed the flocks? You eat the fat, and you clothe you with the wool, you kill them that are fed; but you feed not the flock. The diseased have you not strengthened, neither have you healed that which was sick, neither have you bound up that which was broken, neither have you brought again that which was driven away, neither have you sought that which was lost; but with FORCE and with CRUELTY have you RULED them. And they were scattered, because there is no shepherd: and they became meat to all the beasts of the field...My sheep wandered through all the mountains, and upon every high hill: yea, My flock was scattered upon all the face of the earth, and no one did search or seek after them" (Ezek. 34:1-6).

My motivation for ministry service then moved from being drawn from a slavish commitment to the things of this world and its lies told to me that hinder, hid, and hurt my development into a passionate pursuit of the mystery of the cause of Christ and the building of His kingdom and the discovery of the glory of raising up a community of faith underdeveloped and in need of grace and knowledge.

A number of us who have awakened to the greater spiritual realities have come to see this signal Old Testament passage as a direct prophetic reference to the horrible problems created by the imposition of this world's religious system upon the true people of God. What an indictment of the failed leadership among those who have chosen to depart from the Scriptures and follow the ways of men!

The entire 34th chapter of Ezekiel should be mandated reading for all believers today. Combining that passage with Jeremiah 23 ought to give any open-minded person a clear insight into how God feels about the intolerable situation that has been created by those who have sought to rule over His people. Thankfully, many today have been or are being delivered from the sin of overlordship in the church and its compromising co-conspirator the mismanagement of integrity by those who are appointed or who offer leadership within the culture and commitment of African American families, community and the church. We, who have been so liberated, however, must take definitive steps to prevent this evil practice from becoming rooted in the sincere church.

"Dr. Carter G. Woodson (the creator of Black History week, and author of the Mis-Education of the Negro) wrote: "If a race has no history . . . if it has no worthwhile tradition . . ., it becomes a negligible factor in the thought of the world, and it stands in danger of being exterminated."

The biblical text taught us this as we read the struggles of God's people to keep their passion for Him while living out their promise among the enemies of their image, inheritance and integrity as chosen people of God.

W.E.B. DuBois said, "But the alternative of not dying like hogs is not that of dying or killing like snarling dogs. It is, rather, conquering the world by thought and brain and plan; by expression and organized cultural ideals."

One of these cultural ideas is the use of "Resurrection Thinking" what I call "the incarnational embrace the result of the passionate pursuit of growth through the grace and knowledge of Jesus Christ. Resurrection thinking is the use of a free spiritual thinking process that overcomes what Dr. Cornel West calls the "Nihilistic Threat." The most basic issue now facing the Black church, culture and community: the nihilistic threat to its very existence.

This threat is not simply a matter of relative economic deprivation and political powerlessness – though economic well being and political clout are requisites for meaningful black progress along with spiritual development. It is primarily a question of speaking to the profound sense of psychological depression, personal worthlessness, spiritual neglect and social despair so widespread in Black America.

If one begins with the threat of concrete nihilism, the philosophical doctrine suggesting the negation of one or more meaningful aspects of life, then one must talk about some kind of spirit of conversion. Like alcoholism and drug addiction, nihilism is a disease of the soul that leads to absolute destruction. Any disease of the soul must be conquered by the turning of one's soul. This turning is done through one's own affirmation of one's worth, an affirmation fueled by the concern of others and knowledge and discovery of the hidden fact of God's love. A love ethic or love hermeneutic (interpretation of biblical love) must be at the center of a spirit of conversion.

The goal being to raise up that which now lays in ruins in our lives, homes, communities and churches, repair that which damaged of our spirits, souls and psyches and heal that which has been wounded by making a space for the wounded to be welcomed by the faithful who fully embrace them with the love of Christ and not just superficial religious ideas, actions and attitudes.

In order for free thinking to be actualized a new spiritual state of consciousness (or "Resurrection Thinking") must be realized in the church. In order for this generation to evolve toward the state of fully 'being free" to reach their promise, fulfill their purpose and living a life of self-determination and civilized freedom and prosperity, they must first "spiritually revolt" against the enslaving idea of 'being slaves" and choose to participate in their own "re-creation" or "restoration" through approaching the mystery of life as those committed to living it in Christ-life consciousness and not through flights of fantasy, fright or false perspectives.

The working premise then is that 21st Century African Americans and their houses, communities and churches are spiritually and ideologically stuck at this critical moment in history primarily because they are spiritually existing in a 'none place" of existence and one in-between a "no longer place" of slavery but unable or just plain unwilling to reach a "not yet place" of purpose, promise, productivity and love for the things of God and each other.

As a result we have reached a Red Sea Crossing point of leadership, education and spiritually motivated movement which calls for a paradigm shift in order to move forward in pursuit of the mystery of perfection with clarity, capacity, commitment and consciousness that keeps our dreams from being dashed on the rocks of broken promises, assignments, past bad starts, and past the broken places of mismanaged purpose.

The preoccupation at this point (like that of the people of promise in Scripture) is not with looking back to fight the oppressor but in looking forward to the responsibility of loving Christ and each other through the passionate embrace of the pursuit of the truth we have, resolved to the pursuit of faith in the meantime, and by not dropping the word of truth we've been given as a promise thus, we will not be broken by the process of lack, lost, or languish in an undeveloped and lonely place. We need a process of restoration, refreshing, renewal revival and reconciliation so we can continue to move forward in grace and knowledge, going deeper into the promise of God's mystery of perfection and thus reaching the place of Rerudj.

Revealing the Hidden Mystery

We have a Bible, the Word of God, as we come across words we don't know or principles we are not clear about, even sometimes portions of Scripture we've read many times before, we should dig for richer treasures of its meaning. Pursuing the mystery of perfection is when all of a sudden something from the Word after digging for its treasure just seems to jump out at us. Something is revealed that we haven't seen before. Yes, it has always been there, we just heretofore hadn't seen it or it hadn't been revealed to us before all because we didn't purse it by digging for its hidden, concealed, or perfected mystery.

The king not only leaves a treasure and a map but he also gives us a teacher, someone to help us understand or reveal how to read the map, which is understand the Word. So God told us He would give us the Holy Spirit, who would be our teacher, the teaching priest. "For a long time Israel was without the true God, and without a teaching priest and without law" (2 Chronicles 15:3). So as we pursue the mystery of perfection who is revealing these concealed, hidden things to us? It is the Spirit of God.

The whole idea in all this is that a king doesn't leave their treasure laying around on the surface but in fact it's buried beneath the surface and those who would inherit it will need a map and someone to help them interpret the map someone who values the treasure and is committed to the king whose treasure you are pursuing. So in Matthew 7:6 Jesus says, "Do not give what is holy to the dogs; nor cast your pearls (treasure) before swine, lest they trample them under their feet, and turn and tear you in pieces."

Again, we see that when you have something holy you can't just leave it lying around. It must be buried or concealed because you want your heirs to find it and not those who would trample and misappropriate your treasure or that which is holy. So it says in Proverbs 25:2, "it is the glory of God to conceal a matter." That which God is concealing and that which the kings are searching out is the same Hebrew word, which is 'd'var' or "an utterance," "a saying," a word." So with this in mind, what the text is saying is that it is the glory of God to conceal a Word. Likewise, it is the honor of kings to search or pursue that word. Since we are the ones called a royal priesthood and a holy nation the question then is this: where do we think God would hide a word? The answer in the mystery of His perfection is in His Own Word.

So we don't need to look outside of His perfect Word for the word that He Himself has hidden. He will reveal it to us as we are lead in our pursuit of the mystery by His Spirit and at that moment he wants to reveal to us what He has up till now concealed from us, it will be revealed from within the Word we have not seen before. Yet, the truth of the matter is that it has always been there, it is just that now the Holy Spirit of God is revealing it to you. God in His perfect will is now allowing you to get beneath the surface of the biblical text to behold the mystery of perfection, the hidden treasure within the word. If we are to pursue the mystery of perfection we have to study to show ourselves approved. (2 Timothy 2:15).

One more word concealed in the Proverbs text must be understood, and that word is the Hebrew word "Sartar", which means "conceal." The idea behind this word is that something is being hidden, but it is hidden to provoke someone to passionately go looking for it. In other words, it should provoke someone into pursuing the mystery. The very word that God is hiding is concealed so that you and I would go looking for it. God wants us to pursue the mystery of perfection. This is what we have been talking about all along. We are to pursue that which God has hidden or concealed from the world but has hidden it from us to provoke us to passionately pursue its mystery.

It is like playing the childhood game of hide and seek, where we go and hide because we know somebody is going to come and look for us. We hide to provoke a search. So the object of the game is to hide to provoke someone to come and look for you. This is the idea of the word "Satar" to conceal. God hides things to provoke you and I to look for it; to pursue the mystery with clarity, capacity, commitment and consciousness.

Jesus said to knock and the door would be opened, seek and you will find. Mark 4 said there is nothing that is hidden that will not be revealed. But you have to seek it out. You have to go beneath the surface and dig for it. You must pursue it passionately. Most people fail in spiritual things because they are unwilling to invest in their spiritual life and growth. Jesus Himself said, "Where your treasure is, that is where your heart will follow" (Matthew 6:21). He also made it clear that the secret to success is to passionately seek first the Kingdom of God and His way of being and doing. But seek (aim at and strive after) first of all, His kingdom and His righteousness (His way of doing and being right), and then all these things taken together will be given you besides. (Matthew 3:11 Amplified)

So let's be clear, there are things that God has concealed. This is seen in Proverbs 25:2; Mark 4, Amos 3:7, where it says, "Surely the Lord God does nothing, unless He reveals His secret (the mystery of perfection) to His servants the prophets."These and other scriptures confirm the fact that God does indeed hide things. But the reason God hides things from us is to provoke us to passionately look for them by pursuing the mystery of what is hidden beneath the surface waiting to be revealed. It is revealed to us by the teaching priest the Holy Spirit who helps us to understand the map of the hidden treasure called His Word.

If you are not limited to being religious, or satisfied with your religious ideas, knowledge and growth, and actually want to grow in grace and knowledge of our Lord Jesus Christ, then you must desire to move into a more intimate and personal relationship with Him, then when we pursue the mystery of perfection and draw closer to Him, He reveals through the intimacy of the relationship more and more of Himself, His character, His nature, and begins to entrust to us the mystery of His perfection.

Seeing and Hearing the Mystery

So as Jesus is talking to His disciples in Luke 8:10, "He said, to you it has been granted to know the mysteries of the kingdom of God, but to the rest it is in parables, so that SEEING THEY MAY NOT SEE, AND HEARING THEY MAY NOT UNDERSTAND."

Likewise in Matthew 13:34-35 He says, "All these things Jesus spoke to the multitudes in parables; and without a parable He did not speak to them, that it might be fulfilled which was spoken by the prophet, saying: "I will open My mouth in parables ; I will utter things kept secret from the foundation of the world."

Jesus' stories, or parables, were windows to God's truth. They both reveal and conceal. They conceal from those not seeking the truth, God, or the Kingdom. They reveal to those following Jesus -- his disciples. But the revealing of these messages came through Jesus' time alone with his disciples as he explained God's mysteries to them. The message, however, was hooked into everyday life for them to easily see and hear the mystery, remember it and later to be awakened by these truths when they saw them again in real life.

From this point on, Jesus will put the key focus of his energies and time on helping the disciples see and hear God's mysteries. But the parable of the soils reminded them that they chose whether or not they were soil fit for his seed and whether or not they would be fruitful. For us, the message is much the same: if we want to understand the mysteries of God's Kingdom, we must be willing to spend dedicated and concentrated time with Jesus seeing and hearing the Truth.

The Matthew text is referring to something found in Psalm 78:1-3 which says, "O my people listen to my teaching. Open your ears to what I am saying, for I will speak to you in a parable. I will teach you hidden lessons from our past" This Psalm was written when the tabernacle was moved from Shiloh and the care of the tribe of Ephraim, to Zion in the care of the tribe of Judah. With the move the mystery of perfection transferred the pre-eminence in Israel from the lesser tribe of Ephraim to the tribe most passionate about the worship of God in Judah and was reflective of David (from the tribe of Judah himself) as a man who was in passionate pursuit of God's heart who now was to be the King. They were now to see and hear the mystery expressed through worship.

Though this was the execution of God's mystery of perfection and purpose, it also proceeded from the divine judgment on the tribe of Ephraim, under whose leadership the people had manifested the same sinful and rebellious character which had distinguished their ancestors in Egypt. So God took away His presence and glory from the sinful tribe and placed it where those that were in pursuit of the mystery of perfection were worshiping Him. It took his treasure from the soil of an unfaithful and dispassionate tribe and placed it among a passionate worshiping tribe whose pursuit of an intimate and personal relationship with Him as seen by its leader a man (David) after God's own heart.

So, we see in these passages that Jesus would speak in parables and if you were not seeking a relationship with Him, were not trying to draw close and were not passionately moving forward in pursuit of the mystery of perfection and growing in grace and knowledge of Him as Lord and Savior, if all you wanted was religion, then you were not going to understand. You were not going to find the hidden treasure of the mystery of His perfection.

Those that were close to Him, pursuing an intimate and personal relationship with Him, He would reveal to them hidden things, the mystery of the treasures of His perfection. Matthew 13:10-11, 'And the disciples came and said to Him, why do you speak to them in parables?" he answered and said to them, "Because it has been given to you to know the mysteries of the kingdom of heaven, but to them it has not been given."

Here again, Jesus is speaking to "those who would be with Him," a small intimate group of disciples, who as they sat around Him to intimately draw close to Him, He is saying there are "mysteries" things that have been given to you, and only for you to know. Things about me and my perfection, My purpose and My divine plan and as you draw closer to Me, I am going to reveal them to you. As long as you're with Me, you will both see and hear the truth of these mysteries revealed to you.

The word "mystery" here is from the Greek word "musterion" meaning "A mystery, as in something into which one must be initiated, instructed, before it can be known, something of itself not obvious and above human insight." Mystery is spoken of as things in the New Testament understood as facts, doctrines, principles, etc. not fully revealed, but only obscurely, or symbolically set forth. Its meaning is, not something obscure or incomprehensible, but a secret imparted only to those who have been instructed through seeing and hearing. This was only to disciples, those in personal relationship with Christ, and in passionate pursuit of the mystery of perfection.

So, it is that which is unknown until it is revealed. The word is used chiefly by Paul, who knew well the world of the pagans. Paul accepted this term (mystery) to indicate the fact that, his Gospel message had been revealed to him by the incarnational embrace of the risen Christ.

So in Mark 4:11. Luke 8:10. Matthew 13:11, Jesus said, "It is given unto you to know the mysteries = (hidden truths) of the kingdom of heaven," as in a deeper and more perfect manner than they were made known to others. We now know that to deny that God has hidden things, mysteries, is to deny Scripture which is the Word of God as seen and heard.

How does He reveal these things to us? The answer is by His Spirit or hidden wisdom. The word for hidden he uses is "apokrupto" where we get our word 'cryptic" (having a hidden or ambiguous meaning). Paul speaks of an ambiguous meaning as "hidden wisdom" in I Corinthians – "However, we speak wisdom among those who are mature, yet not the wisdom of this age, nor the rulers of this age, who are coming to nothing. But we speak the wisdom of God in a mystery, the hidden wisdom which God ordained before the ages for our glory which none of the rulers of this age knew; for had they known, they would not have crucified the Lord of Glory. But as it is written: Eye has not seen, nor ear heard, not have entered into the heart of man the things which God has prepared for those who love Him. But God has revealed them to us through His Spirit. For the Spirit searches all things yes, the deep things of God" (1 Corinthians 2:6-10). I believe the

Spirit leads us to pursue the mystery of perfection through the things we see and that which we hear while it is hidden from those who choose the wisdom of this age.

A matter of great concern for some is the issue that mental health professionals describe as "perfectionism." Interestingly, often those who struggle the most with issues of perfectionism are among the most talented people, people who chose the wisdom of this age or whose talents agree with and promote the wisdom of this age. They have often been excellent students, model children, and outstanding people. Some, however, we see become so obsessed or consumed with their every thought, action, and response that they may become far too extreme in their own perceptions of what is expected of them so God hides Himself and the mystery of His perfection. This type of worldly perfection is not the perfection of which we speak.

There is an understandable goal to follow the Savior's direction to "be ye therefore perfect" (Matthew 5:48). While this goal is admirable and appropriate, it is unfortunate that some consider that this perfection must occur through extremes or immediately through the wisdom of the age instead of the passionate pursuit of God's mystery of perfection in Christ-life or living for Christ and His kingdom purposes seen and heard in the revealing to us of the truth.

Patience for the Mystery of Perfection

A careful study of our scriptures teaches us that the notion of being perfect means that we are "complete, finished, and fully developed." Thus, while we should be engaged in the process of perfection, we need to acknowledge that achieving this goal will likely take a long time for all of us and doesn't call for unhealthy or unworthy extremes. The Lord said, "Ye are not able to abide the presence of God now, neither the ministering of angels; wherefore, continue in patience until ye are perfected." What this is saying is continue in patience. The lessons we learn from patience will cultivate our character, lift our lives, and heighten our happiness.

Let us always remember that one of the reasons God has entrusted the priesthood to us is to help prepare us to see and hear the Truth of our eternal blessings by refining our natures through the patience which priesthood service requires. As the Lord is patient with us, let us be patient with those we serve. Understand that they, like us, are imperfect. They, like us, make mistakes. They, like us, want others to give them the benefit of the doubt. Never give up on anyone. And that includes not giving up on yourself. I believe that every one of us, at one time or another can identify with the servant in Christ's parable who owed money to the king and who pled with the king, saying, "Lord, have patience with me." (Matthew 18:26).

In the pursuing the mystery of perfection we learn that patience is far more than simply waiting for something to happen—patience requires actively working toward worthwhile goals, pressing, pursuing, seeking and not getting discouraged when results didn't appear instantly or without effort. Seeing and hearing the truth with patience.

There is an important concept here: patience is not a passive resignation, nor is it failing to act because of our fears. Patience means active waiting and steadfastly enduring. It means staying with something and doing all that we can—working, praying, and exercising faith; bearing hardship like a good soldier, even when the desires of our hearts are delayed. Patience is not simply enduring; it is enduring well!

Patience is a process of perfection. The Savior Himself said that in your patience you possess your souls (Luke 21:19) or, to use another translation of the Greek text, in your patience you win mastery of your souls. Okay, so by applying patience, the issue of self-control might come along naturally as you patiently pursue the mystery of perfection. Two for the price of one!

Patience means to abide in faith, knowing that sometimes it is in the waiting rather than in the receiving that we grow in grace and knowledge the most. This was true in the time of the Savior. It is true in our time as well, for we are commanded in these latter days to "continue in patience until ye are perfected."(Luke 21:19).

To paraphrase the Psalmist of old, if we wait patiently for the Lord, He will incline unto us. He will hear our cries. He will bring us out of a horrible pit and set our feet upon a solid rock. He will put a new song in our mouths, and we will praise our God. Many around us will see it, and they will trust in the Lord. (Psalm 40:1-3).

Impatience, on the other hand, is a symptom of the selfishness of this world. We want it now, and can't wait for it, or don't have time to be patient with it. It is a trait of the self-absorbed. It arises from the all-too-prevalent condition called "center of the universe" syndrome, which leads people to believe that the world revolves around them and that all others are just supporting cast in the grand theater of the drama called you in which only you have the starring role. How different this is from the standard the Lord has set for us as priesthood holders in patient pursuit of the mystery of perfection.

Perfection in Christ is not about adherence to some rigid law it is about God's righteousness living in you. Perfection, the mystery of heavenly perfection which lies before us, has its own shapes and sizes, times and appointments, its own appearance, its majesty touching our inner most soul and spirit and which is our passionate desire as we move forward by His Spirit or hidden wisdom to delight ourselves in the worship of Almighty God. One cannot worship effectively without patience.

Christian worship is to pay honor, give reverence, respect, and glory to the Lord Jesus Christ, to surrender our hearts and humble ourselves before God. These are the things that are to be laid before our Lord. The English word for worship means, "worth ship." It is the state of giving worth, honor or worthiness, and refers to the Excellency of Jesus' character and His dignity. When we as sincere Christians give worship to the God of the Bible, it involves an acknowledgement of Jesus' perfections - His character, His personality, His power, and His purpose.

Under the passionate pursuit of truth and patience and the umbrella of His grace, which comes from the new heart we acquire through baptism of fire and of the hidden wisdom from the Holy Ghost, the concept of walking in perfection is very different from the impossible notions of perfection that have arisen from minds under the bondage of the legalism and the law, and the deception of this world which says that perfection is not attainable in this life and there is only one who was perfect, and that was Christ, whose mission required it. This mindset allows those who won't follow Christ to use the excuse "well nobody is perfect!"

If the perfection admonished in the scriptures for attainment by the saints was not possible to achieve in this life, why, then, did Paul say, "Brethren, I beseech you to be perfect as I am perfect"? (Galatians 4:12.) In fact, his objective in preaching was "that we may present every man perfect in Christ Jesus." (Colossians 1:28.)

Through the school of personal pain and tribulation, Paul himself had learned well the irony that perfection in Christ is brought about precisely because of our patience in weakness, not the other way around, "For," said he, "when I am weak, then am I strong." (2 Corinthians 12:10.)

Recall the time when he prayed three times that his "thorn in the flesh," might depart from him, and the Lord replied to him: "My grace is sufficient for thee: for my strength is made perfect in weakness." (2 Corinthians 12:7-9.) Paul then enthusiastically added, "Most gladly therefore will I rather glory in my infirmities, that the power of Christ may rest upon me." (2 Corinthians 12:9.)

Even in speaking "wisdom among them that are perfect," Paul acknowledged: "I was with you in weakness, and in fear, and in much trembling. And my speech and my preaching was not with enticing words of man's wisdom, but in demonstration of the Spirit and of power: that your faith should not stand in the wisdom of men, but in the power of God." (1 Corinthians 2:6, 3-5.)

"And thus Noah found grace in the eyes of the Lord; for Noah was a patient and just man, and perfect in his generation; and he walked with God, and also his three sons, Shem, Ham, and Japheth." (Genesis 7-10). On the day that he was delivered from his enemies, David likewise acknowledged, "It is God that girdeth me with strength, and maketh my way perfect." (Psalm 18:32; 2 Samuel 22:33.) Several scriptural references refer to the "perfect heart" of David the king (1 Kings 11:4; 15:3; 1 Samuel 13:14; Psalm 101:2; Acts 13:22) and even of those associated with him (1 Chronicles 12:38; 1 Chronicles 29:9). In fact, that description is reserved in connection with him alone, with the two exceptions of kings Asa and Hezekiah. (1 Kings 15:14; 2 Chronicles 15:17; 2 Kings 20:3; Isa. 38:3.)

So as we pursue this mystery of perfection our prayer is from Colossians 4:3 which says, "pray that God would open unto us a door of utterance, to speak the mystery of Christ." In prayer we show our patience or total dependence on God who created all things and us and by whom all things continue to exist. In prayer we give praise, honor, glory and reverence to His name for His greatness and goodness. We recognize Him as the source of all blessings. It is also the outpouring of our hearts desire. In Romans 10:1 the apostle Paul says, "Brethren, my hearts desire and prayer to God for Israel, is that they might be saved." Our prayer must come from our patient hearts.

Prayer to God is only reserved for those who are obedient children of God. We are told in John 9:31, "Now we know that God does not hear sinners; but if anyone is a worshiper of God and does His will, He hears him." There are people whose prayer God will not hear. Isaiah 59:2 says, "But your iniquities have separated you from your God; and your sins have hidden His face from you, so that He will not hear." To allow anything to separate us from the fellowship of God, so that He will not hear our prayers is a very serious matter. It is a sad situation for those who try to pray to God if God will not hear them. But it is their own fault, because they are not patient enough to be obedient to God. They could be obedient if they wanted to be. It they were only patient with the mystery of perfected-ness in Christ.

OBEDIENCE: The third Step in Pursuing the Mystery of Perfection

Our relationship to God requires obedience to divine authority and the function of the Priesthood (John 14:23; 1 John 2:5; 1 Peter 2:5). Jesus answered and said to him, "If anyone loves Me, he will keep My word; and My Father will love him, and We will come to him, and make Our abode with him. (John 14:23)

Obedience to God requires obeying the Word, which requires knowledge of His Word and a willingness to obey. Obedience to God leads to spiritual fellowship with the Father and the Son. The believer in sin cannot have fellowship with God. Sanctification and the filling of the Holy Spirit are required of each believer-priest who desires to pursue the mystery of perfection and sanctified service for His glory. Only the sanctified believer can maintain his relationship with God as a priest. We are not to pursue the mystery unworthily.

The beginning of Jesus' ministry is mysterious to say the least. After thirty years of waiting, God used Mary, to pursue the mystery of perfection through humility and obedience and gave Jesus the signal that the time for miracles had begun. Right in the middle of a group of people-Jesus, Peter, Andrew, James, John, Philip, Nathanael and a entire wedding party and some wine stewards- God tapped Mary, a woman and Jesus' mother on the shoulder and chose her to move forward and pursue the mystery of perfection by obediently lighting the fuse of her own faith and then lighting the fuse of Jesus' purpose and these wine servants service at a wedding ceremony in John 2:5 when she told them to be obedient and "do whatever He tells you to do."

A lot takes place in these two short verses. Jesus gave three specific instructions to the servants. He first told them to fill the water pots. Second, He told them to take some out and third, He instructed the servants to take some to the one who was in charge of the wedding feast. The miracle of Jesus changing the water into wine would have never taken place if the servants had not taken the advice of Mary and been obedient. Then, if not for Mary's obedience the wedding would have been left in a shameful state ... no wine! In verse 5 we read, "His mother said to the servants, 'Do whatever He tells you.'" The mystery of perfection was accomplished when the servants listened to and obediently followed the words of Jesus.

In verse 6 we read, "Nearby stood six stone water jars, the kind used by the Jews for ceremonial washing, each holding from twenty to thirty gallons." The size of these water pots must not be overlooked. These were not mere pitchers found on many restaurant tables today, or sold as bottled water in most of our stores but were large stone containers which held between 20 and 30 gallons each. We are talking between 120 and 180 gallons of water. Filling these water pots was no small task. I doubt they had garden hoses back then and the servants probably had to go to the city well or stream to get the water. Carrying the water on their shoulders for several trips took obedience. The water already in these pots was not necessarily clean for these pots contained bath water used for ceremonial washings. So they had to dump the unclean and replace with the clean.

In Genesis 41:53-57 we read of a time of famine and in verse 55 we read, "When all Egypt began to feel the famine, the people cried to Pharaoh for food. Then Pharaoh told all the Egyptians,

'Go to Joseph and do what he tells you.'" Pharaoh's words are strikingly similar to Mary's. One is a picture of what the world try's to do (unclean) and the other is a picture of what obedience to Christ and the faithful pursuit of the mystery of perfection can do (replace with clean).

Mary's instructions to the servants, "Do whatever He tells you," was good advice back then and also for us today. Jesus did not merely snap his fingers; wiggle his nose, or say, "Presto changeo." But rather, He spoke and the servants followed His instructions. In 1 Samuel 15:22 we read, "To obey is better than sacrifice." The mystery is: Why as believer-priest don't we believe this?

Jesus rescued and saved the wedding feast when He changed the water pot water into wine. In John 2:3 we read again Mary's desperate cry for help, "When the wine was gone, Jesus' mother said to Him, 'They have no more wine.'" Likewise, it is at times like these when we do not know what we are going to do that Jesus wants us to call upon Him. Jesus said in Matthew 11:28, "Come to Me, all you who are weary and burdened, and I will give you rest." The question again is why don't we believe this? Could it be that we just don't believe that obedience reveals the mystery of perfection.

Sometimes we are waiting on Jesus to do something when the mystery of perfection is that He is expecting us to be obedient and do whatever he tells us to do. We are called to do and obey the words of Jesus found in His Word the Bible. We are called to take the steps of faith and obedience operating in wisdom and love. The choice is ours. "Come to Me," are the instructions given.

"Do whatever He tells you to do." Will we choose to act and obey is the question?

"His mother said to the servants, '"Do whatever he tells you.'"These words should become our passionate pursuit in life. I hope they can be woven into the fabric of your life as well. See, that was Mary's mantra. "Be it done to me as you have said" (Luke 1:38), and in the mystery of perfection they soon became "Do whatever he tells you." Mary wasn't just speaking to the servants here. She is speaking to us as well. Do you want to be free from an ordinary life and free to pursue an extraordinary purpose? Then the path is clear, "Do whatever he tells you." Become obedient in the pursuit of the mystery of perfection.

Obedience to God is the key to unlocking the doors to the most exciting life imaginable. It starts when we obediently begin to pursue the mystery of perfection in living our life for Christ.

3

THE HEAVEN AND EARTH PROJECT

The way we have been called and seen ourselves as Christians in the last 10 to 20 years will not be how we're seen and how we'll call ourselves Christians in the next ten years. Some of you will be the next Christians leaders in the next ten to twenty years. You need to be able to take a fresh look at scripture and a fresh read of what God is saying to the world through Scripture in order to be people who can reveal with clarity, capacity, commitment and consciousness that fresh word to the world in new ways.

We have for some reason largely ignored Scriptures such as Ephesians 1:10, 2:10 and 3:10. But if we are to moving forward in pursuit of the mystery of perfection it is imperative that we in our generation not ignore these verses beginning the journey with Ephesians 1;10 where it says, *"God's plan for the fullness of time, was to gather up all things in Christ, things in heaven and things on earth."*

The fact is that we now live in a culture that has separated heaven and earth. With the things of heaven somewhere up there hidden and a long way away from our reality. Somewhere that maybe we'll get to go to one day if we are good. But has not much to do with who we are down here. After all we are just sinners. Sadly, we didn't get this from the bible, as we see in this verse. We got it from the establishment of denominations and the western philosophical and intellectual traditions studied by those who began to lead seminaries and then our churches.

Some two hundred years ago, conveniently, it was decided that we would place God and His heaven up there somewhere and out of sight, so that we could run the world the way we wanted to down here on earth. As a result, we have seen the world, and heaven help us, God, Jesus, and the Bible, and even ourselves as praying Christians in the light of that decision two hundred years later. Since that time we have lived split-level lives. This has lead to a split-leveled eschatology (the word means "the end-times") about where we will go after death. We have come to the conclusion that the mystery of perfection is only found when we leave this world and go to heaven.

But the truth is the bible actually puts this the other way around. The last great scene in the Bible, and God's revelation of the mystery of perfection we are to passionately pursue is not about people being taken away from earth to go to heaven, but it is about the New Jerusalem coming down from heaven to earth so that God's world will be one. Could this be the mystery of God's perfection we have been neglecting, to make heaven and earth one in the New Jerusalem? The Good News is that this has already happened in Jesus Christ. The twin halves of God's creation have already been joined and have been joined once and for all and forever.

Thus, the biblically revealed mystery of perfection is this: "We as followers of Jesus Christ are called to live already in a world in which heaven and earth have come together." It may not look like it when we hear our local and national news. We, hearing this news, are inclined to say, 'if this is what heaven on earth looks like, and if this is all there is to the mystery of perfection, then things have gone sadly wrong." This may be true, but through the power of Jesus Christ, and the mystery of His perfect plan, found in the strength of His Spirit, we are enabled to be people through whom what Jesus launched can actually become a reality.

As the first chapter of Ephesians tells us, we are to be people through whom the power which raised Jesus from the dead will be at work so that signs and aspects of that heaven and earth reality comes to birth within our midst. The problem is that we grew up in a church and many of us are now actively involved with churches and faith communities that simply do not look at truth in this light. Heaven is still like the movie Star Wars, just a galaxy far, far away. We as a result have to just get along as best we can down here on earth where we've come to think that like Darth Vader we are in charge, yet hoping to get to heaven one of this glad mornings so we can fly away to the Death Star. You'll get that when you see the movie again.

We have been robbed - like the man who went down to Jericho and came upon thieves who hit him in the head and left him - of a central truth of our inheritance and the truth of God's mystery of perfection. Jesus taught us to pray *"thy kingdom come, thy will be done, on earth as it is in heaven."* Jesus launched this mystery of the perfection of the heaven and earth project and it will not go away until one day when God's mystery of perfection is fully completed with His return.

Where do we come in then as a result of this truth? When we look in Ephesians 2:10, after the great statement "that we are saved by grace, through faith", we find that there is nothing we can do that earns or merits our salvation. After that however, the

Apostle Paul says, 'we are what God has made us, created in Christ Jesus for good works which God prepared beforehand to be our way of life."

What is so interesting is that the word in the Greek for "we are what he has made us," is 'we are God's poem," "we are God's artwork or masterpiece." "His workmanship the bible says. The good work here is that God has given us many gifts in which we are to not just offer some moral behavior which is often postured as good works, which is important, but the truth is much greater.

The mystery of perfection is that God wants us to be fruitful, to experiment, be innovative, He wants us to be His poem, His work of art in and for the world to behold. To be artist, musicians, poets, dancers, writers, this is our opportunity for good works. While we in the church see this as performing, positioning ourselves to be appreciated and having special gifting and anointing others don't have so we can lord over them with our gifts and talents, God sees our talents and gifts as good works to be used as pictures of His workmanship.

We see art as commerce, things that go on around us and that make life interesting but are really not that essential. Thus, it is easy for us to take creativity, art, music, drama, creative writing out of school, out of church where they used to be expressed and appreciated and out of our homes where they were to be cultivated and see it as less important than promoting the history of the world we like to re-present as truth (history being only the record of struggle) and the lack of the truth of God's heaven and earth project seen in the poems, songs, plays and dramas of our good works as God's workmanship.

Clarity demands that we come to the truth of God's glorious creation, where God made sunlight to spotlight His glorious creation, the music as a result of the symphonic sound of the waves of the seas springing forth from a song He Himself is continuously creating, God made harmony in the wind coming against the tension of the trees, God made fish to swim liquid corridors like dancers twirling and leaping in response to an ancient dance and birds who sing the daily operas of life at every dawning. We are co-creators when we are artists, writers and musicians etc., thus we become the worshipping workmanship of His creative essence and divinely expressed creative faith community. His work of art, created in Christ Jesus to do good works, reminding the world that this is a glorious and marvelous place thus enhancing the beauty of it by our God given gifts, creativity and innovation.

The mystery of perfection is that we are His artwork created in Christ Jesus for those good works which God prepared beforehand for us to pursue as we grow in grace and in knowledge of His purpose, plan and creative power. Then, as this workmanship we must embrace Christ as His disciples and paint a glorious picture for all the world to see as we follow him in pursuit of the mystery of perfection.

So in Ephesians 1:10 the mystery of perfection is revealed as heaven and earth coming together. Then, moving forward on this journey into the mystery of perfection to Ephesians 2:10, we discover the mystery that reveals each of us as God's unique artwork, created in Christ Jesus for every good work. It gives us clarity and a sense of purpose as we understand where we belong in this mystery of perfection. We are to be capable, committed and conscious that we are that place by which not only does heaven and earth come together as a reality in us, but then through us the world sees the beauty of God's perfect plan for our lives expressing the heaven and earth project through our good works.

Then we come to Ephesians 3:9-12 where it says "and to bring to light for everyone (*reveal the mystery*) what is the plan of the mystery hidden for ages in God (*The Mystery of Perfection*) who created all things, so through the church (*the community of God's grace*) the manifold wisdom of God (*the wisdom of God in its clarity, capacity, commitment and consciousness*) might be made known to the rulers and authorities in the heavenly places. This was according to the eternal purpose that he has realized in Christ Jesus our Lord, in whom we have boldness (*moving forward*) and access (*passionately pursuing*) with confidence through our faith in Him."

God's wisdom has many facets and aspects much like the intricacies of a precious diamond when exposed to the light of inspection. Now these intricacies are being revealed for our clarity, the building up of our capacity, to sincerely commit ourselves, consciously to this heaven and earth project in pursuit of the mystery of perfection in Jesus Christ our Lord.

4

THE INCARNATIONAL EMBRACE

*I*n pursuing this mystery, Jesus said to His disciples "in Mark 8:34-35 "He called the crowd with his disciples, and said to them, "If any want to become my followers, let them deny themselves and take up their cross and follow me. For those who want to save their life will lose it, and those who lose their life for my sake, and for the sake of the gospel, will save it."

So many people still misunderstand Jesus. So many church folk still cannot tell what he stands for and what the ethical results can be from pursuing the mystery of perfection as a follower of Jesus Christ. And almost all church members have lost sight of the humanity of Jesus instead they only want His divinity which lets them off the hook when it come to being Christ-like.

Looking at one of the instances where this misunderstanding comes to mind we follow Jesus into the mystery as he comes to the Garden Of Gethsemane where He spends the last night of his earthly life in anguish, praying. Do you remember what he prayed? "If it is possible, father, let this cup of suffering pass from me; nevertheless, it is not what I want but what you need that must be done." Again, I offer you another picture of this mystery of perfection as seen in the anguish of the Lord's suffering yet embracing the will of God for His life.

Jesus of Nazareth, the teacher and prophet and favored one of God who really did have a choice that night of following through with his vocation or falling away. This was not a superhuman, unfeeling super hero; this was in the words of the first ever Christian sermon recorded in the book of Acts 2:22-23 by Peter: 'Jesus was a man attested to us by God through whom God did wonders, signs, and deeds of power. A man whom, after he was executed like a criminal, was raised from death by God and whom God made Lord and Messiah."

The Bible always has started with the humanity of Jesus before it talks about his divinity, but that is still very confusing for many as it has been since his death and resurrection. We continue to be confused by the heaven and earth project in the mystery of perfection. When we look at the story of Jesus what is it that we learn? What do we clearly understand? What are we conscious of? What are we committed to?

Sincerely, looking at the biblical text, we see Jesus invite people to turn in a new direction—to repent and trust in the good news he is bringing. We see that he spent most of his ministry in a very small area around the north end of the Sea of Galilee and much of that time in the town of Capernaum where he had a home or stayed in the homes of two brothers, Peter and Andrew. Jesus was able to stay committed to His faith community why it is those who say they are His followers can't seem to stay committed to theirs?

He taught in the synagogue in Capernaum and much of his ministry was spent making people well and whole—in healing people. My question is this, "are the wounded still welcome in church along with the left-out, leftover and left behind? Or is church now only a place for those who have arrived in Jesus and need the amenities of life, special parking, padded pews and assigned seats, childcare, coffee shops, one hour worship services, fifteen minutes limits for preaching, ministry and the invitation to Christian discipleship, ATM money machines for convenience, or just the use of direct deposit, programs for every affected life issue, problem or need, television church so the lazy don't have to come at all?

Jesus very quickly ran into conflicts with the religious leaders who did not think he was properly pious or reverent enough because he did not observe all the rules and laws they emphasized and because he was always associating with the wrong kind of people—outcasts, the wounded, demon possessed, sinners, impure, lepers and prostitutes, messed up people like you and me. In fact, he thought and taught that those impure, sinful people were just as welcome as the most religious leaders—an idea that scandalized them and continue to scandalize the sincere church that loves with a pure heart, good conscience and sincere faith today. Some people we've come to believe are just not welcome in our churches. But are they welcome in Jesus'? Does He still embrace them?

By chapter three of the gospel of Mark these religious leaders had begun plotting to kill this troublemaking Nazarene prophet named Jesus. How dare he promote the heaven and earth project and move among us offering this mystery of perfection by embracing the wounded, left out, left over and left behind as a picture of faith, hope and love.

What else do we learn as we read each chapter of this earliest and shortest of all the four gospels? Jesus, pursuing this mystery taught with authority, clarity, commitment and a special heaven and earth as one consciousness in contrast to the other rabbis. By the way, Rabbi was the term most often used to address Jesus, and rabbi means teacher. But as one scholar has said Jesus is still a stranger in the midst of his own people and many people still have a third grade Sunday School stereotype of a gentle Jesus meek and mild instead of the fiery prophet /teacher who, in the gospel of John, uses his passion as a teaching instrument for change and not only drives the money changers (ATM machine and direct deposit ministries) out of the temple when he gets to Jerusalem but does so with a whip he makes himself and turning over their tables! Talk about turning the class out.

Teacher, fiery prophet, friend of the outcast, healer of the hurting - has anyone seen this Jesus lately in our churches and individual ministries or even in our prophetic proclamations? Are the wounded still welcome and do the faithful still have fellowship with this Christ or have we shaped our own god and now look to another after our own understanding? Have you encountered His heaven and earth project and His incarnational embrace in your life and church?

The truth is that Jesus picked his disciples from common folk whom he met as he taught around the shores of the Sea of Galilee—fishermen and even a hated tax collector. He invited these twelve to do the same thing he invites us to do—not to worship him or to admire him or to show up in church once in a while and give him a tip instead of a tithe, or offer an A&B selection, singing, swinging, sweating and swearing in fruitless disobedience to Him and call it being faithful—but to follow him, to imitate him, to be like him, to be his learners and students; to encounter the heaven and earth project and receive His incarnational embrace. And these good friends who had the privilege of spending three years learning from him—what kind of students do you think they were? What kind of commitment did they make? What kind of capacity did they express? What kind of clarity did they have about this Jesus they were following?

They proved to be remarkably dense, at times foolish and certainly unclear about the mystery of perfection being expressed to them by Jesus! He often displayed his disappointment with them and his discouragement at how long it was taking for them to understand the life of service and sacrifice that he stood for—yes fulfilling rewards as well in the here and now—but selflessness first. Even as he was taking them toward Jerusalem in the last weeks of his life, several of them were arguing on the way about which of them he liked best and who was going to have the most status when Jesus conquered the Romans and became an earthly king. He had to stop them and straighten them out and tell them that to be great, they had to learn to carry the tarnished cross of sacrifice and learn to be servants and that he himself had come not to be served but to serve. In Latin this is called "Ministrare non ministrari" – To serve and not be served.

He promised, to those who would come after him, not status and glory, but he promised what he said in Mark chapter 8: "If anyone wants to come after me—it is a daily choice—If you want to come after me, you must forget yourself, take up a cross and follow me." The cross is a symbol here of self giving and of self denial. It is the tarnished cross of the heaven and earth project where it is better to serve than be served.

And then there is a promise: whoever does this will find life but whoever tries to hold on to life and focus only on themselves will be losers. This is the turning point in the gospel of Mark and is one way of summarizing Jesus' message revealing the mystery of perfection as embracing Jesus as the way, the truth and the life and become a winner.

As a basketball player growing up in Southern California one of the people I looked at as an example of perfection was John Wooden the legendary former coach of UCLA who recently passed away at the age of 99 – and is one of the winningest coaches in basketball history. Recently, while reading a copy of His book it noted how he led his team to win 88 straight basketball games between January 1971 and January 1974. His teams were perfect for three years. Since then no one has even come close to that record. He won 10 NCAA championships at UCLA and no one has come close to that either.

At the time of his passing he knew the whereabouts of 172 of the 180 players whom he coached. Many of them would still call and check in on him and secretly hope to hear some of his simple life lessons like the following:

"Discipline yourself and others won't need to. Never lie, never cheat, never steal. Earn the right to be proud and confident. Never score without acknowledging a teammate. Treat your opponent with respect. One word of profanity and you're through for the day."

In a word, embrace life as a winner and not as a loser! No UCLA basketball number was ever retired under his watch. He said, "What about the fellows who wore that number before?

Didn't they contribute to the team?" He didn't throw away his players and neglect them like so many coaches of young athletes today caught up in the worldly aspect of winning at all cost and not the development of winners in life through the development of their character. Admittedly, he was a square and hopelessly "old fashioned" and some would say out of fashion but he was someone I grow up looking at as a model of integrity and virtue as a former basketball player. We all wanted to play for him because he was a winner!

When All America center Bill Walton showed up with a full beard, he knew rebelliously it was against Coach Wooden's policy – "Facial hair takes too long to dry and you could catch cold leaving the gym" Wooden would say to his players.

Bill Walton said about his beard defiantly, "It is my right." Coach Wooden asked Walton if he believed that strongly and Walton said he did. Coach said, "That's good Bill. I admire people who have strong beliefs and stick by them. I really do. We're going to miss you here at UCLA Bill." Walton shaved off that beard that day, and from then to the day Coach Wooden died, once a week, Bill Walton would call coach Wooden to tell his coach that he loved him. Coach Wooden, knew about the heaven and earth project of sacrifice and incarnational embrace. His embrace of winning ways was a mystery of perfection to those without an understanding of his intimate and personal relationship with Christ that guided his pursuit of excellence. But he knew what he was and that was just a disciple, a follower of the heaven and earth project of Jesus. He used his talent as a coach to become God's workmanship.

There is a quote from the winningest basketball coach of his time that echoes what we hear in the timeless words of Jesus because part of John Wooden's value system is that he was a disciple, a follower of Jesus of Nazareth, one who passionately pursued the mystery of God's perfection. He tried to do what Jesus invites each of us to do—to learn from him, to imitate him, to follow him, and to make that our first priority in life. To encounter the heaven and earth project and receive His incarnational embrace daily thus pursuing the mystery of perfection by moving forward and following Him, taking up the tarnished cross of sacrifice daily becoming God's workmanship, His poem His master coach.

Wooden's quote:

"There is only one kind of a life that truly wins, and that is the one that places faith in the hands of the Savior. Until that is done, we are on an aimless course that runs in circles and goes nowhere. Material possessions, winning scores, and great reputations are meaningless in the eyes of the Lord because he knows what we really are, and that is all that matters."

"If anyone wants to come after me, "Jesus said, " let them forget self, take up a cross and follow me, for it is when you lose yourself in me and in my good news, that is when you will find life." Right after Jesus says this in Mark's gospel, chapter 8, he sets his face toward Jerusalem and moves forward, further into the mystery of perfection. He has had some success in his ministry in Galilee but he knows now that he needs to confront the corruption and the empty religion he has seen around him and he must do that in Jerusalem, the center of that bureaucracy, and he knows the cost involved in that confrontation; it will cost him his life, but to be faithful to God and to his calling to bring people close to God's incarnational embrace he must do this. In pursuing this mystery so must we.

5

THE TARNISHED CROSS

Whenever God is at work there is a cost. Whenever we're called to follow Jesus there is a cross. Whenever we discover that we are gifted in particular ways and realize that God wants us to use these gifts for His glory rather than for our own self aggrandizement, then there will be something that causes us pain. Paul talked about it as the "thorn in the flesh." This thorn was given to him to keep him from being overjoyed or become self indulgent about the abundance of revelation that was provided to him by Jesus' call on his life to go and be an apostle to the gentiles.

Pursuing the mystery of perfection and taking up the tarnished cross causes pain but do not be afraid when God calls you. God is calling each of us to be who we uniquely can be. He wants to use your unique gifts for His glorious purpose according to his perfect plan. This is the awesomeness of our Christianity. On one hand we are all the same because we are all one in Christ. However, moving through the process of pursuing the mystery of perfected truth with clarity, capacity, commitment and consciousness of another point of view, we soon discover than each of us are absolutely unique, created in Christ Jesus to bring into the world that which you and only you can bring. Yes, there may be many things that you and I are capable of doing. But we must carefully commit ourselves with clarity, to the consciousness necessary to understand the truth that there is something you and only you at the moment can do.

However difficult or painful it is to give up those other things that you might want to do, you have got to do this thing as God's workmanship even if it means bearing the tarnished cross of sacrifice and selfless service.

This selfless service was seen in the life of a local church pastor the late Pastor Shelter White of Emanuel Missionary Baptist church in San Dimas, CA. He had served the Lord and His church for over fifty years. Recently, while writing this, Mother Dorothy White, his widow sent for me to come to her home. It was then that she gave me as a gift, a cross continuously worn by Pastor White for over forty years. The cross, purchased at a time in their ministry where with a large family, and little income he could not afford a real gold cross, so he brought one that really had no worth or earthly value. Now tarnished, and worn from forty years of service by this man of God, she felt that his appreciation for the ministry service I am humbled to offer here at Imani Temple Christian Fellowship in Pomona, expressed the heartfelt love he had for the Lord and his appreciation for me and the calling on this ministry. She closed by saying that he called me a true general of the faith. Wow!

As we forge a path through the challenges and attacks to reach our ultimate goal of becoming a more excellent ministry and a sincere church we move forward bearing the tarnished cross fulfilling the goal of Christ as expressed in Matthew 6:10. This is part of what we have come to call the Lord's Prayer. Most of us who have grown up with a Christian background have prayed this prayer more times than we can remember, yet we have not often realized what we were praying for: 'Your kingdom come." The prayer goes on, 'Your will be done on earth as it is in heaven."

So, the prayer is saying, 'Your kingdom come on earth." The ultimate goal of God for this present age is the coming of His kingdom on earth under his leadership as the chosen King, the Lord Jesus Christ. I believe that He will actually have an earthly kingdom and that He will reign as king. I believe this is the only solution to the problems of this world and should be the focus of every church leader . . . How shall we serve the King and Kingdom? My answer is by accepting the Tarnished Cross of leadership, putting no value on the earthly positions, presentations, and proclamations of our service to Him. But humbly and graciously presenting our bodies as living sacrifices, holy and acceptable unto Christ as our reasonable service to Him as the King and His soon coming Kingdom (Romans 12:1-2).

This has been my church's guiding and governing theme scripture established when the ministry was started some twelve years ago and continues the focus and purpose of ministry and service to this body of Christ called Imani in pursuit of the mystery of perfection, as we, the servant leaders of the Lord's church, seek to prefect the saints for the work of ministry to Him and His kingdom.

Some people would say Jelani, you are a dreamer, that I am talking about pie in the sky. Yet, after all these years and now many more witnesses than even I realize, I think the people who can imagine that man can resolve his own problems are the real dreamers. We are probably further away from resolving the problems of the world at this time than ever before. So how can anyone persuade us that it is going to change through the efforts of man and those that do are dreaming and need to "WAKE UP!"

There is only one hope it is through the tarnished examples of living sacrifice we offer as believers, followers, disciples, and servant leaders in pursuit of the way, will, Word and wonder of Christ Jesus. Every committed Christian needs to line up and present themselves to this hope by bearing the tarnished cross of faithful service to the purpose and plan of the Lord Christ Jesus.

"And the world is passing away, and the lust of it; but he who does the will of God abides forever." (I John 2:17). God's will is not going to change! If there has to be any change, it is our wills. If we as leaders and believers align our wills with the will of God, if we make the purpose of God our purpose in life, we will be as unshakeable and undefeatable as the will of God. "He who does the will of God abides forever," The crucial issue then for every person, especially those attempting to serve with the tarnished cross of faith is: Are you aligned with God's will? Is God's purpose your purpose?

For many churchgoers and leaders sadly, the answer is not so. They are involved in all sorts of religious presentations and activities, earthly and worldly concerns, and their hearts grow cold to the demands of the will of God. Sadly, they have lost sight of the goal, the end purpose, which is the establishment of the kingdom of God on earth. Not just the making of oneself comfortable or celebrated. But crucifying your flesh and bringing down every thought that is not of God.

What makes a leader according to God's will anyway? Is it rank; Status; Celebrity; Clout; Style; Gifting; or Charisma? Is leadership automatically bestowed by a box on the organizational chart or the letterhead? Where do positions and power figure into the formula for serving God? And what is the ideal model for leaders? Is it the corporate CEO model of the worldly system now so popular that it has become adopted in many of our churches as a proper leadership structure? How about the military commander model? Or even the head of state model? When Mother White said her husband called me a General of the church what did he mean really by that?

Jesus answered all those questions for me and I offer the answers to you here. He offered them in just a few words. His views on leadership are conspicuously out of step with the conventional wisdom of our age. He said, 'You know that the rulers of the Gentiles lord it over them, and those who are great exercise authority over them. Yet it shall not be so among you; but whoever desires to become great among you, let them be your slave –(let them wear this tarnished cross – my addition) – just as the Son of Man did not come to be served, but to serve, and to give His life a ransom for many" (Matthew 20:25-28). *"Ministrare non ministrari"*, to serve and not be served.

According to Christ, then, the truest or sincerest kind of leadership we can offer demands service, sacrifice, and selflessness. A proud and self-promoting person is not a good example of leadership and is not a good leader by Christ's standard, regardless of how much clout they might have and are able to wield. Leaders who look to Christ as their leader and their supreme model of leadership humbly will have servants' hearts. They will exemplify sacrifice and faithfully and humbly wear the tarnished cross of service.

I realize these are not characteristics most of you associate with leadership, but they are essential qualities of a "BIBLICAL APPROACH" to leadership, which is the only kind I'm interested in and you should be too. Notice if you will, by the way, that when you play the whole tape, that Jesus was expressly teaching Christians to approach leadership in a different way and from a radically different point of view than the leaders of this world. It is foolishness for Christians to assume (as so many of you do) that the best way for Christians to learn leadership is from worldly examples.

Lastly, there is a crucial reason for this whole thing. Is it this" Leadership for the Christian always has a spiritual dimension. The duty of leading people carries with it certain spiritual obligations. Whether we are talking about the pastor of a Christian church or a stay at home mom whose sphere of influence extends no further than her own children. All Christians (ALL) in every kind of leadership are called to be 'spiritual leaders.' We all (All) need to remember that the leadership role is a spiritual responsibility, and the people we lead are a stewardship from God, for which we will one day be called to give an account" (Matthew 25:14-30).

If you truly understand your accountability before God as a leader, you can begin to see why Christ portrayed the leader as a servant and why, Christ is demanding that you and I, as His servants, and soldiers on the battlefield for the Lord, assume the posture and personality of the cause by wearing a tarnished cross mentality and positioning ourselves as living sacrifices, holy and acceptable in service of the King.

He was not suggesting, as many of us want to suppose, that lowliness alone is the essence of leadership and neither am I. There are plenty of humble, meek, tenderhearted, servant-minded people who are not leaders. A sincere tarnished cross bearing leader inspires followers. Someone who has no followers, or who lead people away and not to the blood stained cross and banner of Christ can hardly be called a leader.

So while it is certainly true that leadership demands a servant's heart, exemplified by the metaphor of a tarnished cross worn over it, it is by no means the case that everyone with a servant's heart is thereby a leader. Simply put, for those who wear the tarnished cross we are looking for someone whose life and character motivates people to follow. The best kind of leadership derives its authority first from the force of a righteous example, and not merely from the power of prestige, personality or position. By contrast, much of the world's "leadership" is nothing more than manipulation of people by threats and rewards. That is not true leadership; it is exploitation. Sincere leadership seeks to motivate people from the inside, by an appeal to the heart, not by external pressure and coercion. For all these reasons, leadership is not about style or technique as much as it is having the character enough to wear

. . . A Tarnished Cross!"

6

LIVING THE MYSTERY OF THE TABERNACLE

*I*f we are to pursue the mystery of perfection we will inevitably come to probably the greatest of all mysteries in the Scriptures and that is the mystery of the Tabernacle of Moses built in the wilderness. By omitting the tabernacle of Moses in our pursuit of the mystery of perfection, we actually neglect a powerful and necessary tool that God prepared for us to understand the mystery of the work of Christ on the cross.

What is it about mysteries that so intrigue us? In part because they peak our sense of curiosity, the meaning is never apparent initially, and takes some digging beneath the surface for the truth to be unfolded and revealed. The things of God that are not entirely clear cause us to pursue them with more focus and passion and by doing so patiently and obediently we grow in grace and in knowledge of the mystery of perfection.

It is the tendency of the post-modern or contemporary reader of Scripture to neglect the details of the Old Testament to instead focus our attention on easier aspects of the New Testament instead. In this wise, we tend to overlook the 50 chapters devoted to the pattern of the tabernacle seeing it all as irrelevant and quite simply rather boring and un-useful for our modern purposes. But just like the parables of Jesus bring to life His teachings, the revelation of the tabernacle in the wilderness of Israel's wanderings and wonderings serve to illustrate spiritual patterns and concepts that come alive in the New Testament.

This mystery of the tabernacle begins by first introducing a wayward band of wanderers, former slaves held until recently in bondage in Egypt and now having fled their captors find themselves in the wilderness following a mysterious unseen and unknown God. Although now free from Pharaoh they were yet slaves mentally, emotionally and spiritually. The whole concept of God was confusing to them at this time and all that was familiar was the ways and gods of their former masters in Egypt.

This is a picture of each of us as we come out of the bondage to this world, confused and unfamiliar with the mystery of God's perfection and how to have an intimate and personal relationship with God. We are unable to approach a holy God as sinful men and women. We are more familiar with the things of the world than we are with the things of God. We must never forget that it was at the foot of the mountain of God, Mt Sinai that these same Israelites bowed and worshipped a golden calf. The prosperity teachings, the influences of personalities and false teaching, all are preparing us to build today's Egyptian cows.

The truth of the matter is that the tabernacle is God's picture of what was required for man to approach an intimate and personal relationship with Him. It showed the children of Israel, and today shows us in its example, God's holiness that we may as sinful men and women approach this holy God, and that we must come to God in the mystery of His perfectly prescribed pattern. The tabernacle not only prescribes the mystery of God's perfection in its pattern of approach, but also we realize His forgiveness as we move forward growing in grace and knowledge through the concepts of how to worship and seek Christ in Spirit and in Truth.

As John the Baptist, declared 'Behold the Lamb of God who takes away the sins of the world in John 1:29; when he saw Jesus, it is no mere coincidence that at the same time sheep where being slaughtered for the evening sacrifice highlighting the sacrificial system of the Jewish faith up to that time. In true mystery of perfection fashion the activity of the brazen altar in the tabernacle system helped to give wise witness to what was to happen on the cross and the significance of Christ's death and the redemption of mankind from the separation of a Holy God by sinful man. The result was our receiving His incarnational embrace and coming into Christ-life as we grow in grace and knowledge of our Lord and Savior Jesus Christ entering the Holy Place of humble service on our way to the intimacy of a personal encounter with God in reaching the mystery of perfection in the Holy of Holies.

It is impossible to talk about living the Christ-life or understanding the true nature of serving God without encountering the clarity, capacity, commitment and consciousness of service expressed by the priesthood originally established in God's commands to Moses for its service in the Tabernacle. Thus, the Tabernacle is the physical embodiment of the heaven and earth project 'a copy and shadow" Hebrews 8:5 calls it, to teach us spiritual truths.

The whole Jewish system of worship was a compacted example of their faith in salvation from sin. While we have many wall sculptures, temples and gods in Egypt, there was only one God and one Temple in Hebrew beliefs. Every act of the priest in the shadows of the mystery of service, as he went in and out, was an example or prophecy of the Savior's work when he would enter heaven as the repentant sinner's substituting High Priest in the heaven and earth project.

The construction of the Tabernacle was the good news of redemption in examples and figures as the Lord's object lesson or classroom for the "children" of Israel. Being surrounded by the idolatry of the nations who inhabited the Promised Land and burdened down from years of bondage in Egypt the Israelites had only a dim understanding of the faith of their fathers and the faithfulness of Almighty God. They had become children in comprehension, and in order to reach them, God taught the gospel in a way that their senses could grasp. It was through this object lesson of the Tabernacle.

The concept of sin and Savior goes hand in hand as biblical themes. There once was a being that God had placed over all of his created beings. This highly placed being, named Lucifer, became high minded and self-centered in his own imagination which led him to want to take the place of God himself. A created being wanted to take the place of his creator. From that time on, from ages past, Lucifer sowed thoughts of doubt and lies among other angelic beings. All the universe knew that sin would bring death but Lucifer told them in essence when he insinuated: `No! You and I were created immortal. If you die, it is God who killed you.'

"And the serpent said to the woman, Ye shall not surely die: For God does know that on that day you eat of this fruit, then your eyes shall be opened, and you shall be like the gods, knowing good and evil."(Genesis 3:5)

With such untruths about God Lucifer succeeded in bringing 1/3 of the angelic host on his side, according to Revelation. 12:4. But what is God's answer to the lie of Lucifer about death? Sin is the transgression of God's law and thereby separation from God, the source of life. It is like unplugging the battery charger. The radio will still play as long as there is sufficient energy coming from the battery, but once the battery charge is used up the radio will play no more, all sounds from it will die. Sin has occurred and we live, so to speak, on battery power today. But a day of restoration was promised, restoration for those who repent of their mistakes, change their life and claim the Savior's redemptive power. Some day there will be no more sin and sinners, for God promised to restore the world to the way it was originally planned to be. It was the mystery of perfection.

All God's beings have their own free will and so did Lucifer. Sin therefore was first born in his heart. When we go back to the wilderness tabernacle we see, when we discern the glorious gospel of the Savior that Christ is the perfect expression of God's plan shining within the mystery of the establishment of the Tabernacle.

God's Design in the Sanctuary

There is a new television program being advertized for the upcoming fall television season entitled: "The Event." One of the greatest events in the bible is the giving of the Ten Commandments on Mt. Sinai within the hearing of the Israelites. That is why we read, "For ask now of the days that are past, which were before thee, since the day that God created man upon the earth, and ask from the one side of heaven unto the other, whether there has been any such thing as this great thing is, or has been heard like it? Did ever people hear the voice of God speaking out of the midst of the fire, as thou hast heard, and live?" (Deuteronomy 4:32-33)

How glorious an event the proclamation of God's law was is underscored by the record stating that tens of thousands of holy angels attended this event as well. We read, "And this is the blessing, wherewith Moses the man of God blessed the children of Israel before his death. And he said The Lord came from Sinai, and rose up from Seir unto them; he shined forth from mount Paran, and he came with ten thousands of saints: from his right hand went a fiery law for them." Deuteronomy 33:1-2.

It was evident, before Israel could appreciate the mystery of God's perfecting, they must know and understand the meaning, the grandeur, the majesty, and the purpose of God's mystery of perfection. So we must know this before we pursue the mystery as well. These events have been written down long ago and it is unwise to ignore them. The Bible represents God's recorded testimony for man. Like a nation publishes a law and it is up to the citizens to read it or not, they are held responsible for its demands, so too, and much more so is God's published law, His entire scriptural record, for which the universe is responsible. Such a book is the Bible. We are held responsible for all its contents.

That is why Satan ceaselessly sows seeds of doubt, disappointment and delusion in the soils of our souls. We must not pay attention to his continuous criticism, attacks and lies. We must give God our undivided attention by reading and learning His Word growing in grace and in knowledge of the Lord Jesus Christ and moving to consciously living a life in Christ, the Christ-life. Doubt makes struggle more difficult than the test of faith intended. The Bible teaches we must learn to wait upon the Lord, 2 Chronicles 13:10; Isaiah 30:18.

Moses was on Mt. Sinai on two occasions, each lasting 40 days and nights, Exodus. 34:1-4, 28; Deuteronomy 9:9. During this time he fasted, he neither ate food nor drank water. The whole time his attention was fixed on the mystery of perfection in the visions as God was showing Moses how to build the Tabernacle and conduct the ministries to Him there. Once having experienced this close communion with God, he continually pursued the truths of this mystery during the remainder of his ministry. Based on these occurrences Jesus said the words, "Blessed are they which hunger and thirst after righteousness: for they shall be filled." Matthew 5:6. It is therefore no idle assurance that from the heavenly manna and the water of life springing from the rock which followed Israel, refreshing satisfaction for the soul is derived.

Day and night, for nearly 12 weeks altogether without physical sustenance, the prophet Moses was intensely observing what was demonstrated before him. He passionately pursued the mystery of perfection and to Moses was being revealed the sanctuary in heaven. His mind and thoughts were concentrated on what was being shown to him. Repeatedly the admonition was given: "Look! See! Watch! Make all things according to the pattern, Exodus 25:40; Numbers 11:23; 27:12; Ezra 8:29.

God impressed upon the mind of Moses the scenes which were being revealed to him. He was commanded to make such careful and strict observations that every detail he was to construct would be in perfect agreement with what was revealed to him.

Notice that the Tabernacle and its purposes did not come to man by his study, or by his investigation, or by his research; It came to Moses directly from God by prophetic (vision) revelation. It was for this purpose that Moses was called to climb upon the mountain to be with God in the mystery of perfection.

Christianity is centered on the substitutionary death and resurrection of Jesus Christ. Jesus Christ suffered this death just outside the gate, near ancient Jerusalem to offer redemption to individuals from the consequence of sin in our lives. Above and beyond God's love and forgiving attitude toward us, He wants to actually heal us from the sin itself and from its consequences.

In this sense His achievement on the cross was complete, finished seen in the activities of the Outer court and the approach to the Brazen Altar of sacrifice. But the mystery of perfection was not completed as far as arriving at `throne/ark/mercy seat' is concerned? It is the book of Hebrews which opens up to our understanding the work which Christ began after His blood was shed on Calvary and after He ascended to heaven (Hebrews. 8:1-2; 9:1-28;) to make application of His sacrifice. It implies a move forward from the sacrificing of our sin to serving God as his holy vessels to receiving redemption as we arrive in the Holy of Holies as we encounter the beauty of holiness with the presence of God.

And so we found that the architectural layout of the tabernacle put the symbol of the death of Christ on the cross in its very center. In the Outer court we find the `Altar for Burnt Offerings'. Most Christian churches have a working knowledge of this part of the mystery of the meaning of this aspect of biblical teaching.

However, the significance of the second central spot, where the `Ark of the Covenant' topped by the `Mercy Seat' stood (Exodus 25:17-22; 26:34), is perhaps not given adequate time and insightful study in the width and depth of this mysterious architectural arrangement filled with spiritual meaning. And so we find that many Christian churches stop at the cross and do not proceed to understand the place where at times God set up His throne between the Cherubim angels on the Mercy Seat/Throne, Exodus. 25:22; Numbers 7:89. Since both, altar and throne, are biblically emphasized, `these become important topics in our pursuit of the mystery of perfection.

Let's take a moment here to express the mystery of perfection as symbolized by living in the Holy Place of the Tabernacle, where every furnishing corresponds to an aspect of the Spiritual life that must be perfected. The Tabernacle was a mystery set forth to investigate (from a spiritual viewpoint) how man, who in Truth is Spirit, fell into the trap of believing himself to be flesh and became imprisoned in the limited realm of the senses. Our goal is to develop a dialogue in pursuit of finding a key to this mystery of perfection using the picture of the Tabernacle as our personal life enriching experience.

What is the goal of salvation? The truth of the matter is that the goal of salvation is not to populate heaven. Did you know that the mystery of God's goal is to have on earth a corporate Priesthood who will make visible His Love, through the wisdom of obediently pursuing the mystery of perfection?

This first requires that we understand that Christ alone is our priest who offers access to God's grace. Only on the basis of his sole priesthood is our priesthood established. We too are priests, because everything Christ has is ours through the mystery of the blessed exchange of our justifying faith. Thus we are priests as Christ was priest.

Here is where the mistake emerges in the role of the priest within our understanding. It is so easy to slip into thinking that we have access to God as Christ had access to God. The priesthood of Christ ends with our priesthood for ourselves. Hence you have the erroneous notion of the Priesthood of *Each* Believer: every Christian as his or her own priest. This is like the mistake we also make with being His temple. Many want to believe they don't have to be obedient because they are his individual temples in which God dwells in and as so don't have to answer to anyone, come under authority or even attend to the purpose and plan of God by becoming a part of His body the church. We become do-it-yourselves Christians instead of temples of Christ constructed after the pattern God showed us in His Word.

But the principle in both examples is not that we procure access to God for ourselves through Christ, but rather that we are priests for one another as Christ is for us. This is the logic of the "as": in as Christ was a priest for others, so I am a priest for others. On the basis of the priesthood of Christ, all those who believe in him become priests for their family, friends, neighbors, and even enemies. As Christ suffers for others, we wear the tarnished cross of sacrifice and so we too are required to suffer for others. As Christ offers forgiveness, so we offer forgiveness to others. As Christ is our access point to God, so we become others' access point to Christ and the pursuit of the mystery of perfection.

So the Priesthood of All Believers does not imply do-it-yourself Christianity. Rather, we are empowered by Christ's priesthood to be priests for one another. Thus, the sincere Church is the community of priests, a community of grace continually offering Christ to one another. And the Priesthood of All Believers is an unmistakably spiritual/cultural/communal activity that incorporates Christ, culture and community.

Our goal of pursing the mystery of perfection is to find what is buried inside man... the true Spiritual identity of man; the mystery of the priesthood of all believers. This is where you and I become vitally important! Every Christian has heard the Holy Spirit's statement; "Christ in you, the hope of glory" (Colossians 1:27). The mystery of perfection, or let's call it the Father's light within you, the hope of glory" (Colossians 1:27). The Covenant, the perfect intent of God, can only be complete in Christ -- God's Covenant was originally made with His Anointing. The original covenant was between the Father and His Son, which was later illustrated in His Covenant with Abraham.

Before there was any written Bible Moses and Israel (some 2 million people) had arrived at Mt. Sinai after their Exodus from Egypt, which had been 430 years since the Covenant made with Abraham in Genesis 12. As they pursued the mystery of perfection they finally came to Mt Sinai the mountain of God. In Exodus 25:8, The LORD said, "And let them [Israel] make me a sanctuary...." The Tabernacle, in the Wilderness ... as a prophetic designed illustration of the Tabernacle found in Revelations 20:3, "Then I looked and saw that the Temple in heaven, God's Tabernacle, was thrown wide open."

God, on Mt. Sinai, gave Moses the intricate and detailed plans for the pattern of the mystery of the Tabernacle. The Tabernacle was a very complex wood (overlaid with gold) building -- housed under 3 tents and surrounded by a white fence – encompassing 7 specific pieces of furniture. The family of Levi was separated for the work of this Tabernacle. And the family of Moses' brother, Aaron (and four sons), were appointed as its Priests and Teachers.

The materials, the colors, the construction, the room divisions, all represent how the spirit of God, in man, operates -- making visible the government of the invisible God and His mystery of perfection.

The Tabernacle was constructed specifically as a house for the Ark of the Covenant and is a house constructed for worship.

The Ark and its contents were symbols of the Presence of the Covenant God. The Tabernacle was a center for teaching true worship. Learning how to appreciate the value and appropriate the worth of our covenant is Worship. God said, "And there I will meet with you, and I will commune with you from above the mercy seat" (Exodus 25:22).

The purpose of our worship is to glorify, honor, praise, exalt, and please God. Our worship must show our adoration and loyalty to God for His grace in providing us with the way to escape the bondage of sin, so we can have the Christ-life He so much wants to give us. The children of Israel were delivered out of the bondage of Egypt to come into the presence of God for the purpose of worshiping Him. The martyred deacon Stephen while preaching in Acts 7:7 said, "'But I will punish the nation that enslaves them,' God said, 'and in the end they will come out and worship me here in this place.' The nature of the worship God demands is the prostration of our souls before Him in humble and contrite submission. James 4:6, 10 tells us, "God resists the proud, but gives grace to the humble. Humble yourselves in the sight of the Lord, and He will lift you up". Our worship to God is a very humble and reverent action.

Jesus says in John 4:23-24, "But the hour is coming, and now is, when true worshippers will worship the Father in spirit and in truth, for the Father is seeking such to worship Him. God is a spirit and they that worship Him must worship Him in spirit and in truth." It doesn't say we can worship God anyway we want, but we "must worship Him in spirit and in truth". The word "must" makes it absolute. There is no other way we can worship God and be acceptable to Him.

The word "must", expresses "an obligation, a requirement, a necessity, a certainty, and something that must be done". When "must" is used it means that it is not optional. Therefore 'worship' is not an option. Here the word "must" is expressing that in spirit and in truth is the only way to acceptably worship God. God seeks true worshippers, and He identifies them as those who sincerely worship Him in spirit and in truth". Worshipping God in spirit and in truth is a serious matter which must not be taken lightly. If we have any regard for our own souls, we will want to make sure we are worshipping God according to His pattern of perfection.

Since God is the object of our worship, He and He alone has the right to determine how we are to worship Him. We read in Jeremiah 10:23, "O Lord, I know that the way of man is not in himself, it is not in man who walks to direct his own steps." We are not granted the option of directing our own ways in religion. God is the One who we look to for guidance and direction in our lives.

Our very best in worship is due God and is prescribed by Him in the Bible. The worship God has prescribed is the only way we can be pleasing to Him in this life and finally attain everlasting life with Him in eternity. The Christian's worship is of the greatest importance.

Worship is a time when we pay deep, sincere, awesome respect, love, and fear to the one who created us. Acts 17:24-25 says, "God who made the world and everything in it, since He is Lord of heaven and earth, does not dwell in temples made with hands, as though He needed anything, since He gives life, breath, and all things."

Levels of Intimacy

Does God have favorites? Is God a respecter of persons? No, Scripture teaches that we, not God, determine our own level of intimacy with Him by whether we are seen moving forward in pursuit of His mystery of perfection or whether we pursue the things of this world. We have all been extended the open invitation to "fearlessly and confidently and boldly draw near to the throne of grace, the throne of God's unmerited favor to us as sinners, that we may receive mercy for our failures, fears and frustrations and find grace (Hebrews 4:16). At this moment, each one of us is as close to God's throne of grace as we choose to be.

Before the children of Israel were given the instructions to build a tabernacle God has to deal with their understanding of the levels of intimacy required in approaching Him. Looking first at God's dealings with the Israelites beginning in Exodus chapter 19, we see four levels of intimacy that we can choose to have with God as we pursue the mystery of perfection.

Moses went alone to the top of the mountain to speak with God, but God established borders or boundaries at three more levels on the mountain to which others could also ascend in order to draw near to Him. These boundaries coincided with the corresponding level of maturity and commitment by those desiring to move forward to pursue intimacy with Him.

The first boundary or level of intimacy was at the foot of the mountain: And the LORD said to Moses, "Behold, I come to you in the thick cloud, that the people may hear when I speak with you, and believe you forever." So Moses told the words of the people to the LORD. Then the LORD said to Moses, "Go to the people and consecrate them today and tomorrow, and let them wash their clothes. And let them be ready for the third day. For on the third day the LORD will come down upon Mount Sinai in the sight of all the people. You shall set bounds for the people all around, saying, "Take heed to yourselves that you do not go up to the mountain or touch its base. Whoever touches the mountain shall surely be put to death.'" (Exodus 19:9-12)

Then the Lord invited Aaron, Nadab, Abihu, and seventy of the elders of Israel to come closer to His mountain habitat and worship at a distance, thus demonstrating a second level of relationship with God. Joshua was allowed to climb up to the third level before Moses left him to approach the Lord alone establishing the fourth level as an intimate and personal relationship with God.

Exodus 24:9-17 explains: Moses and Aaron, Nadab and Abihu, and the seventy elders of Israel went up and saw the God of Israel. Under his feet was something like a pavement made of sapphire, clear as the sky itself. But God did not raise his hand against these leaders of the Israelites; they saw God, and they ate and drank. The LORD said to Moses, "Come up to me on the mountain and stay here, and I will give you the tablets of stone, with the law and commands I have written for their instruction." Then Moses set out with Joshua his aide, and Moses went up on the mountain of God. He said to the elders, "Wait here for us until we come back to you. Aaron and Hur are with you, and anyone involved in a dispute can go to them."

When Moses went up on the mountain, the cloud covered it, and the glory of the Lord settled on Mount Sinai. For six days the cloud covered the mountain, and on the seventh day the Lord called to Moses from within the mystery of the cloud. To the Israelites the glory of the Lord looked like a consuming fire on top of the mountain.

Why would God let some people into a certain level of His presence, but allow others to come closer, and some, like Moses, to see Him face to face? In Exodus 32 we see that the level of commitment each group demonstrated to God parallels the level of intimacy each group experienced on God's mountain. In the mystery of perfection we decide what depth of His presence we will enter by our level of obedience to His instruction in our lives.

To everyone at the first level, God was saying, "I'm coming to visit you, but you can only come this far into the mystery of perfection and My presence." And they were comfortable remaining at the foot of the mountain where they could hear God's voice as He talked to Moses. They didn't move beyond that boundary because to them God looked like a consuming fire.

Remember, this was the same group of people who later sharing their gold jewelry made a golden calf to worship because they grew tired of waiting for Moses to come back from spending time with God. It is amazing to see that they worshiped the "Bling" God had given them when they left Egypt instead of the Covenant Light that shines with intimacy in His presence (Exodus 32:1-6).

Aaron was among the priests and elders who ascended to the second level and were privileged to see the beauty of God's feet (Exodus 24:9,10), yet he later helped the children of Israel prepare an altar for their unholy sacrifices. And his sons, Nadab and Abihu, who shared this encounter with God, eventually lost their lives for making an unauthorized sacrifice to Him (Numbers 3:4). Those who are at this level often compromise their positions and promises in their responses to the commitment of the pursuit of faithfully serving the mystery of perfection.

Joshua, an aide to Moses, was allowed to ascend into the third level of intimacy with God where he watched Moses enter the cloud of God's presence. We see Joshua's humility and dedication to serve the Lord as we watch him faithfully assist Moses whenever he was needed. When Joshua wasn't serving his mentor Moses, he could be found praying (Exodus 33:10-11). He was one of the twelve spies sent into the Promised Land, and one of two who came back with a good report of faith in God's ability to give them the land (Numbers 13). God chose Joshua to replace Moses when it came time to take the people into the land God had promised them based on his response at this level of pursuit of the mystery of the perfection.

In Deuteronomy 4:36 and Nehemiah 9:13 the Lord had spoken from heaven, as if Mount Sinai was enjoined to heaven and Moses peered into third heaven! It was on this mountain that Moses saw the heavenly realities (Hebrews 8:5) which prompted him by the Lord's guidance to create a tabernacle to match the perfected reality he was privileged to witness. This mountain, covered in fire, was like that of the fiery bush seen in Exodus 3, and of course pointing further back to the fire on the holy hill, guarding Adam and Eve from the garden and the tree of life in it. So, the Mount was a boundary between Heaven and earth.

But, despite the mountain being such a boundary and that Moses himself had reaped such wonderful privileges from the Lord in the pursuit of the mystery of perfection which was not exclusive to him, but also given to the Israelites (v.13 – they shall come up to the mountain!), the Israelites remained at the foot of the mountain They trembled at the sound of the trumpet, rather than rejoiced. Indeed, they had treated Moses as someone special, despite Moses and Aaron both insisting that they themselves are not the mediator gods. Today, we see this as people of God worship the personalities of their pastor/priests instead of moving into a committed personal relationship with God for themselves. After all, we as pastors did not die for you we are just called out and placed in your life to lead you to Him and anything we do to take your eyes and affections from Him we will be held accountable for by Him.

God through this intimate dialogue on the mountain beginning first establishes a tabernacle for God to dwell in and then, while there, with his finger of authority wrote Ten Commandments for His people to pursue as the mystery of perfection. The unseen, invisible Lord (the Father – Colossians 1:15) would not be seen in this form again until Luke 3:22, 9:35; John 12:28-29 with Jesus' incarnational entrance and embrace.

Exodus 20:2 begins: "I am the LORD your God, who brought you out of the land of Egypt, out of the house of slavery." Indeed, this is past tense: He brought the Israelites out of Egypt. He saved the Israelites.

This is similar to his statement in Exodus 19:4 about His act of salvation, and NOT their act of self-salvation.   And the

Israelites' faith stems very much on this repeated refrain of Him being the one who brought them out of the land of Egypt. It is a statement meaning to show trust, hope, and faith. God himself requires of them their obedience in living as God tells them to, for their lives were ransomed by God, for God. Likewise, our life is life lived for Christ through Christ.

In giving The Ten Commandments they are not about bondage life; or works-salvation. Rather, they are very much about liberation after salvation; it is about living a new life, the Christ-life, under God's command, rather than returning to their old life. It is all about God's completed saving act and our response as people already saved to that wondrous act, setting up the third level of intimacy with Him through our obedience.

Moving Forward in the Mystery of the Tabernacle

Now we come to this holy sanctuary which God wants the Israelites to make exactly (Exodus 25:1-9). The details undoubtedly contribute much to the mystery of knowing more about Jesus. If the truth of God is in the details, the very details which He provides for us, then we should spend time considering them as greater opportunity for worship. As modern day readers of the bible, we tend to skim over the detailed texts especially those of the Old Testament and rather focus our attention on simpler texts in the New Testament. It is tempting to overlook these detailed sections of Scripture and their contribution to understanding the mystery of perfection buried like treasure within them.

Just like Jesus' parables serve to illustrate and bring His teaching to life, so the Old Testament visual texts and testimony serve to illuminate the many mysterious spiritual concepts we soon found critical to our New Testament understanding. With this in mind, omitting the details of the construction of the Tabernacle given to Moses we may actually be neglecting the powerful and necessary tool that God prepared for us to understand the mystery of the perfect work of Christ on the cross.

It was in the tabernacle that God perfectly pictured what was required for man to become right with Him. The detailed commands that God gave the Israelites for the pattern of setting up the tabernacle, demonstrates to us God's character in order for us as sinful man to approach a Holy God. We discover by the mystery of perfection in the construction of the dwelling in the wilderness for God's presence, God's own prescribed way of coming into His presence.

First and foremost, the contributions come from "every man whose heart moves him" there is a sense of voluntary servant hood -"*Ministrare non ministrari*" – To serve and not be served. in the contributions being offered to the design of the tabernacle here, as opposed to the rebellious self-serving building of the golden calf earlier, through the contributions of the unfaithful, but also implies that this is no legalistic enterprise. Only for those whose hearts are circumcised and are open to moving forward into the mystery of perfection and obeying God may participate.

(a) Gold, silver, bronze (v.3)

(b) Blue and purple and scarlet yarns and fine twined linen, goats' hair, tanned rams' skins, goatskins (v.5)

(c) Acacia wood (v.5)

(d) Oil for the lamps, spices for the anointing oil and for the fragrant incense (v.6-7)

(e) Onyx stones, and stones for setting, for the ephod and for the breastpiece (v.7)

The above 5 groups of items are used for the making of this holy sanctuary called The Tabernacle. Their significance is not apparent yet, and will only come to light when we see how these items are being used - nonetheless, remind yourself that God is in the details, the item used, the way in which the items were contributed (by a moving-heart) and the way in which the items will be implemented only add to the perfection of the mystery.

The first thing we should note is that The Ark of the Covenant was to be placed inside the Holy of Holies - the Most Holy Place and is mysteriously mentioned first. This detail is interesting: why is the Ark of the Covenant, the Table for Bread and the Golden Lampstand mentioned before the Tabernacle structure in Exodus 26? Surely any architect would start with the structure, before going into the furniture of the structure?

The Tabernacle revealed the complex design of the spiritual body of man and the detailed pattern which allows the indwelling God to manifest (reveal) His character. It is a blueprint "design" of the Spirit "body of the Christ," i.e.; "The Word was made flesh, and dwelt [Tabernacled] among us" (John 1:14). The LORD said; "And let them make ME, a sanctuary...."

The "Mercy Seat" should be considered as a throne - in 1 Samuel 4:4 the language used is that the Ark of the Covenant is enthroned between the cherubim. No doubt, this ark also symbolized the throne of the Father in heaven – (Daniel 7:9-10 and Revelation 4:1-3). Wouldn't it be proper to first enthrone God before building a structure for Him to dwell in? Likewise, we can only worship God properly if first we make Him Lord. First in our lives and everything we obediently structure called life.

Then there is Isaiah 37:16 who speaks of the LORD who dwells between the cherubim; and Ezekiel 1:4-5, 26-28 speaks of four living creatures and the throne of God. It is therefore quite clear that we should consider the meaning of the ark of the covenant, on which is the Mercy Seat lid, to be considered as a throne imitating the throne in heaven.

Above the Ark of the Covenant and the atonement cover, The Mercy Seat God appeared in His glory in "unapproachable light" (1 Timothy 6:16). This light is sometimes referred to as the Shekinah glory. The word *Shekinah*, although it does not appear in our English bibles, has the same roots as the word for *tabernacle* in Hebrew and refers to the *presence of the Lord*.

The Mercy Seat represented the connecting link between heaven and earth. In this mystery of perfection we call this the Heaven and Earth project. The two cherubim angels both faced the center of the chest made of acacia wood, in token humility and reverence bowing and in symbol representing the entire heavenly hosts and how they intently regard the perfect law of God and the plan of redemption. We can only imagine how intent the angelic hosts are observing everything having to do with salvation and the resolution of sin in this world is brought out several times in the Bible especially during the time of the birth and ascendance of Jesus Christ back into heaven and is presented in all four gospels: Matthew, Mark, Luke and John.

We read words like: "The angel of the Lord appeared unto Joseph ... And the angel answering said unto him, I am Gabriel, that stands in the presence of God; and I am sent to speak unto thee, and to shew thee these glad tidings. ... And Jesus said unto him, Verily, verily, I say unto you, hereafter ye shall see heaven open, and the angels of God ascending and descending upon the Son of man. ... And he was in the wilderness forty days ... and the angels ministered unto him." Matt. 1:20; Luke 1:19; John 1:51; Mark 1:13.

The presence of these angels emphasizes the importance of these events and goings on, also doubly emphasized by Jesus using the word `verily' twice. It appears that when Jesus spoke something twice he was speaking to the mystery of perfection in the heaven and earth project.

Who was the angel Gabriel (Daniel 10:21; Revelation 1:1)? We may not be far off to say, that the angel Gabriel who stood in the presence of God, holds now the position which Lucifer abandoned when sin was found in him. We do well to take heed of the instruction presented in these passages in their entire context, for the angels wanted to witness how the problem of sin was going to be resolved and apparently aid in its resolution somehow according to the mystery of the heaven and earth project. For this reason alone we probably should not leave one facet of the details of the mystery of perfection in this great event unnoticed and proclaimed for we were created just a little lower than the angels, Psalm 8:4-5 and as such ought to watch and pray as well.

Because the ark was God's throne among His people, it was a symbol of His presence and power with them wherever it went. There are quite a number of miracles recorded in the Old Testament surrounding the ark: With the presence of the ark, the waters of the River Jordan divided so the Israelites could cross on dry land, and the walls of Jericho fell so that the Israelites could capture it (Joshua 3:14-17, 6:6-21).

Yet the ark could not be treated with irreverence because it was also a symbol of God's judgment and wrath. When the Israelites fought their enemies the Philistines during the time of the prophet Samuel, they disregarded the commands of the Lord and took the ark out to the battlefield with them, "summoning" God's presence. God caused the Philistines to win the battle and "the glory departed from Israel, for the ark of the Lord was taken" (1 Samuel 4:22).

However, God showed His power to the Philistines when He caused their idol, Dagon, to fall to the ground when the ark was placed next to it, as though it had fallen down in reverence to God Almighty, the God of Israel and several Philistine cities were plagued heavily when the ark was in their midst (1 Samuel 5). Ultimately, the ark was returned to Israel through the proper profession of worship by David's pursuit of the mystery of perfection.

What may seem strange to us today is that, hidden in the special golden box representing God's presence were not treasures and precious gems, but three unlikely items: a jar of bread, a stick and two stones. What were these curious keepsakes and why did God want them in His ark?

A Jar of Bread, A Stick and Two Stones.

These three articles represented some of the most embarrassing and disgraceful events in the history of the Israelites. First, the pot of manna: "This is what the Lord has commanded: 'Take an omer [portion for one man] of manna and keep it for the generations to come, so they can see the bread I gave you to eat in the desert when I brought you out of Egypt.'" (Exodus 16:32)

God had provided this bread-like food called manna for the Israelites when they grumbled during the wanderings in the wilderness asking "what is it?" It was bread from heaven! He continued to provide the food daily and faithfully, but the people were not one bit thankful. They complained and wanted something else. The pot of manna was an uncomfortable reminder that despite what God had provided for them, the Israelites had rejected God's provision.

Second, Aaron's staff that had budded was mysteriously placed in the Ark: representing "a sign of the rebellious" when the people, out of jealousy, rebelled against Aaron as their high priest. To resolve the dispute, God commanded the people to take 12 sticks written with the names of the leader of each tribe and place them before the ark overnight. The next day, Aaron's rod from the house of Levi had budded with blossoms and almonds. God confirmed his choice of Aaron's household as the priestly line.

"And the Lord said to Moses, 'Put back the staff of Aaron before the testimony, to be kept as a sign for the rebels, that you may make an end of their grumblings against me, lest they die.'"

(Numbers 17:10) The staff reminded the Israelites that on more than one occasion, they had rejected God's authority.

Third, the two stone tablets with the Ten Commandments: God had chosen the Israelites as His special people. For the Israelites to qualify for that distinction, God had demanded one thing. They must obey His Law, the Ten Commandments. This was a conditional agreement:

"Now if you obey me fully and keep my covenant, then out of all nations you will be my treasured possession. Although the whole earth is mine, you will be for me a kingdom of priests and a holy nation." (Exodus 19:5-6)

The Israelites had said rather passionately, "All that the Lord has spoken we will do," in response to God's covenant (Exodus 19:8). But how did they fare in fulfilling their end of the contract? The sad report is miserable. It was impossible for them to keep the Ten Commandments perfectly. Over and over again, they violated God's holy Law, and God made it clear to them the consequences of their sin by sending plagues, natural hazards and foreign armies upon them. The stone tablets in the ark were a reminder that the Israelites had rejected God's right standard of living.

These three articles were preserved in the ark throughout Israel's history as an unpleasant symbol of man's sins and shortcomings, a reminder of how they rejected God's provision, authority and right standard of living. It pointed to man as a helpless sinner.

The Central Theme

Moses had gone into the mountain sanctuary to speak to the Lord, instead the Lord spoke to Moses. Our question may be, how open are we to hearing the voice of God when He is speaking to us? (Hebrews. 4:14-16). What things keep us from a fuller communion with God?

Divine messages were sometimes made known to the high priest by a voice from the pillar of the cloud. Other times a light would shine upon the angel on the right indicating approval or the angel on the left, indicating disapproval, this is implied in Exodus. 25:22. But the Good News was the Glory of God kept showing up!

"Then a cloud covered the tent of the congregation, because the cloud abode thereon, and the glory of the Lord filled the tabernacle." Exodus 40:34. "And all the children of Israel murmured against ... `Would God that we had died in the land of Egypt ... let us return ...' ... then Moses and Aaron fell on their faces ... rebel not ye against the Lord ... But the congregation (of the Israelites) said stone them with stones. And the glory of the Lord appeared in the tabernacle of the congregation before all the children of Israel." Numbers 14:2,5,9,10. "... the glory of the Lord appeared unto all the congregation." Leviticus 9:23; Numbers 16:19,42; 20:6.

Hannah's prayer incidentally mentions ... "He raiseth up ... to make them inherit the throne of glory ..." 1.Samuel 2:8.

"... for the glory of the Lord had filled the house of the Lord." 1 Kings 8:11; 2 Chronicles 5:14.

"Now when Solomon had made an end of praying, the fire came down from heaven, and consumed the burnt offering and the sacrifices; and the glory of the Lord filled the house. And the priests could not enter into the house of the Lord, because the glory of the Lord had filled the Lord's house. And when all the children of Israel saw how the fire came down, and the glory of the Lord upon the house, they bowed themselves with their faces to the ground upon the pavement, and worshipped, and praised the Lord, saying, For he is good; for his mercy endureth for ever." 2 Chronicles 7:1-3; Micah 7:18,19.

"And the glory of the God of Israel was gone up from the cherub ..." Ezekiel 8:4; 10:4.

Underneath the cherubim angels between which the glory of the Lord appeared, inside the Ark, was enshrined the law of God. That law pronounces death upon the transgressor, but above the law was the Mercy Seat indicating or pointing forward to the mystery of perfection in the sacrificial atonement provided by the death of Jesus on the cross, so that pardon could be granted to repenting sinners who would turn away from sinning and become obedient to the Lord. When we do, the Glory shows up and grace and mercy together with righteousness and peace come together and kiss each other.

"Surely his salvation is nigh them that fear (respect, reverence) him; that glory may dwell in our land. Mercy and truth are met together; righteousness and peace have kissed each other." Psalm 85:10.

There is no question that the crucifixion of Jesus Christ is a central point in biblical teachings and Christian beliefs. This is abundantly made clear in the Old Testament and especially also the New Testament. But the sacrifice of Christ on the Cross is in the past, God, at some point, wants to direct our attention to His Throne, and the mystery of perfection before which we all must appear. The time for our attention toward His Throne in His Sanctuary is now! These are not new teachings. They were taught in the Bible all along we just did not faithfully study God's Holy Bible enough. The question, Why was the sacrifice in the sanctuary not the end but the beginning of the sanctuary service, is already answered here. Our first question may be this: Is the centrality of the altar/cross imagery in the Old and New Testament also made clear on the subject of the centrality of the throne in the New Testament?

From the Old Testament we know that the high priest would enter the Most Holy Place of the tabernacle sanctuary once each year on the Day of Atonement that means, the high priest served inside this Most Holy place rarely while he went inside the Holy place every day. Just because we come to church doesn't mean the Glory will show up every time or in some churches at all. The question is how are we serving Him when we get there? It is in the faithful serving and giving of honor to God that prepares us for Him to reveal the mystery and personally show in all His Glory.

Since the inner veil separating the Holy from the Most Holy the veil did not reach to the ceiling, the glory of the Lord, when manifested above the Mercy Seat, was partially visible from the Holy Place or Inner Court. When the priest offered incense before the Lord, he looked toward the ark; as the burning cloud of incense rose toward the ceiling, the divine glory descended upon the Mercy Seat and filled the Most Holy place representing the Glory and the Divine Presence.

This burning incense, ascending with the prayers of people, represents the love, merits and intercession of Jesus Christ, His perfect righteousness, which through faith is imputed (accounted for) to His people, and which alone can make the worship of sinful beings like us acceptable to God. This was a time of intense interest to the worshippers who had assembled at the tabernacle. As they searched out in their minds their sins in silent prayer to confess them, their petitions ascended with the cloud of incense before the Lord, while in faith they laid hold upon the shed blood of the sacrifice as we do today in silent prayer at home or in church.

While the burning of incense, slaying of sacrificial animals were done away with at the cross, we, who "nailed" Christ to the Cross by our sinning, still need to pray, search out our sins, exercise faith, confess and repent, but not to appease an angry God, No, but to satisfy the demands of God before the universe of fallen beings, who are interested to know that Satan will be forever conquered, so all who are thus reconciled as citizens of God's kingdom are assured of peace and love forever. We ought to practice what we pray. Perhaps that may lead someone to show an interest in where you worship and the desire to join in the pursuit of the mystery of perfection there.

This experience of looking into the mystery of perfection through the experience of the Tabernacle helps us to discover a personal identity with the "dwelling place of God." Ninety-nine times the Tabernacle is referred to as the dwelling place of God.

'Know you not that you are the temple of God and that the Spirit of God dwelleth in you?" (I Corinthians 3:16). "Behold, the Tabernacle of God is with men" (Revelations 21:3).

The Tabernacle is the mystery of perfection in Jesus, nothing more, nothing less. He is the gate, for He is the Way. He is the curtain into The Holy Place, for He is the Truth. And He is the Veil into the Holy of Holies, for He is the Life. No man cometh unto and into the Father, except he come by this same pattern, The Way, The Truth, The Life.

Jesus is the Altar, for it is his Sacrifice that reconciled you to God. He is your substitute seen in every lamb, ram offered. When God in the mystery of perfection placed Him in the game, in your place, He became you, and the person you thought you were, has now been replaced by Him, the person you are. So He is playing in our place, in the game called life as we live in the mystery of the Christ-life.

He is the fire on the Altar, for it is His passion that is consuming you like Holy fire so that your greatest desire is to please the Father and lives to do His will with clarity, capacity, commitment and consciousness.

He is the Laver, He wants to wash and cleanse you with His Word. And as He told Peter, 'If I don't wash you, you have no part in me." When He has washed you, you will look into the looking glass of the Laver (made from the eyeglasses of the Israelites) and see nothing but His Glory, in your face: "Behold I see as in a glass."

He is the Candlestick, for He is the Light of the world. The Candlestick is the illuminated Word. There is no other Light and there is no need for any other light; for He, as the Word, is the light of you – the temple. He is the Shew bread or the Presence. He is the Bread that came down from Heaven. He is the Wine. He said, "If you eat My flesh and drink My Blood, you shall never hunger nor ever thirst nor ever die." He is the Golden Altar, He ever liveth to make intercession for you. "I will pray the Father" He said.

He is the Veil, which is taken away in Him. When His flesh was torn on the Cross, the Veil in your temple was torn, from top to bottom, from the Spirit to the Soul, from Heaven to Earth. He took away the middle wall of separation. He is the Mercy Seat. By His grace, He paid your price. He purchased your debt. His Blood marked – Paid in Full – for you, with two witnesses the Cherubim hovered above the Mercy Seat in the Father's presence.

He is the Ark of the Covenant. The Ark was made to look like a coffin. He was buried for you and you were buried with Him. And He, in you, gives Life to that part of you that was separated from God and died. He is the resurrection power in Aaron's rod. He budded and blossomed and brings forth fruit in manifested life, in you and I, and for you and I, as the mystery of perfection. And He is also the hidden Manna and once you've tasted it, there is never ever any food on Earth like it. You will say, with Him, "I have food that you know not of."

He is even the Covenant Law, seen in the two tablets of stone, written in your heart. He is you, in Oneness, for you and as you fulfilled in the Law. He in you is the Spirit of Life, the Christ-life. He is your Spiritual passion for life and the pursuit of the mystery of perfection and the passion to share His life with others. It is His Spirit which giveth Life.

As believers in Christ we do not look at the Tabernacle in particular, or some tent in the wilderness as our destiny or even the Bible in general, as a history lesson. Our journey is to find in the wisdom in the Scriptures and see the application of the events, situations and, circumstances, in the things we face in life every day.

In this portion of the journey it would be good to remember that we are not sent to teach anything new here. We are sent however to pursue the mystery of God's perfecting work in us to help you remember those things you were taught in the beginning... to you who were chosen in Christ before the foundation of your world. What we want is for you to discover that 'learning' regarding this mystery is simply the wisdom of 'remembering.' And that we are spirit prepared here for a pre-arranged earthly purpose to fulfill the mystery of God's perfecting work.

Growing in Grace

and Knowledge

You Never Leave

This God character he don't ever leave
He doesn't even live on Earth
Yet he has been with me since birth
Even when I stray and sin
He is there to welcome with a grin
Although his eternal presence is confusing
Because being with me is something He is choosing
No He still won't leave me be
But now I know it's because He has planned my ultimate destiny

___Zaina Goggins

7

GROW IN GRACE AND KNOWLEDGE

Grow in grace - That is, in every Christian aspect, temper and desire. There may be, for a time, grace without growth; as there may be natural life without growth. But such weakened and sickly life, of soul or body, will end in death, and every day draw nearer to the unfulfillment of the mystery of our pursuit of Godly purpose. Health is the means of both natural and spiritual growth. If the remaining evil of our fallen nature is not crucified daily, it will, like an evil growth in the body, destroy the whole man.

We are healed by the wonderful gift of Grace, when we accept and then experience God's loving forgiveness in our lives, it produces harmony within our relationships and repairs the hurts and hindrances of our past to walk in the fullness of the mystery of God's perfecting love. Encountering God's grace changes lives forever and His transforming mercy can awaken in each of us the freshness of the experience of being in God's favor and presence as He pursues us with His unquenchable love.

If we through the Spirit do crucify the deeds of the body, (only so far as we do this,) we shall live the life of faith, holiness, and happiness. The end and design of grace being purchased and bestowed on us, is to destroy the image of the earthy, and restore us to that of the mystery of heavens perfect purpose that we might live a fully redeemed life in Christ what we call here Christ-life. And so far as we do this, it truly profits us; and also makes way for more of the heavenly gift of the mystery of perfection, that we may at last be filled with all the fullness of God.

The strength and wellbeing of a sincere Christianity depends on what our soul feeds on as the health of the body depends on whatever we make our daily food. If we feed on what is according to our nature, we grow; if not, we suffer and die. The soul is of the nature of God and nothing but what is according to his holiness can agree with it. Sin of every kind starves our souls and makes it consume itself away. Let us not try to change the order of God's mystery of perfection or we shall only deceive ourselves. It is easy to forsake the will of God and follow our own ideas, perceptions and desires but this will bring on an emptiness of the soul.

It is easy to satisfy ourselves without being possessed of the holiness and happiness of the gospel. It is easy to call forth these feelings of self satisfaction and then for them to oppose faith in Christ and lead us to the false promises and a life gone astray.

Feelings are the divine considerations of the Holy Ghost shared in the heart of him that truly believes. And wherever faith is, and wherever Christ is, there are these blessed divine considerations framing our purpose and feelings. If they are not in us it is a sure sign that though the wilderness became a pool of refreshing restoration and rivers of living water flowing out of our inner most being the pool has dried up and is now become a wilderness again. This has been affected by the lack of the knowledge of Christ and the mystery of perfection in Him. That is the faith which is the root of it all and the reason for our pursuit.

The one thing we all need to do more is to grow in the love of God and in His grace and knowledge. And that means in learning how to let these rivers of living water flow out of our innermost being. Yet, how many individuals believe this today?

Both 2 Peter 3:18 and Colossians 1:9-10 clearly show the importance of growing in knowledge. On the one hand, we are called to knowledge of the Truth – the unalterable revealed Truth that contains no error – and we are told to hold fast to that Truth. On the other hand, we are admonished to grow in grace and knowledge. By this we come into the Lord's perfect will for our lives.

TRINITY: The Loving Community of Grace

*"Grace never casts nature aside or cancels it out,
but rather perfects it and ennobles it."* (Pope John Paul II)

Moving deeper into the mystery of perfection we acknowledge and agree that in order to accomplish the objective of pursuing the mystery of perfection we must be led and directed by our Lord and Savior, Jesus Christ, empowered by the Holy Spirit, in full grace and knowledge of the wonderful mystery of God, the Father, perfectly expressed in the Trinity. God, who is revealed to us in Scripture and who lived among us in Jesus Christ exists as a loving community of grace in the Trinity, God in three persons.

The Father, Son and Holy Spirit each relating to one another with grace, love, mutual submission and unity shaped, shared, served, synergized and surrendered in purpose and power – the Holy Spirit to the Son and the Father, and the Son to the Father. Together, they fully express the mystery of perfection. Marvelously, this triune God (the Father, Son and Holy Spirit) invites us to move forward in order to grow in grace and knowledge as we pursue the mystery of this perfection in intimate relationship and purposeful embrace to participate in partnership as we encounter this loving community of grace and His community of faith called the church.

Biblical truth is the foundation of our pursuit of this mystery of perfection and on which our faith and the transformation necessary to live the fully redeemed life in Christ depends.

Moving forward into the mystery of perfection is the challenge to journey with the Trinity, the community of grace, to encounter that which is greater than what we have heretofore imagined or experienced as people and communities of faith.

In short, the pursuit of the mystery of perfection is seeking spiritual direction and purpose to experience the fullness of the majesty of the Father, the grace and incarnational embrace of the Son, Jesus Christ, and the power, purpose and promise of the joy of the Holy Spirit. Through preparation, partnership and purpose these three progressive steps form the dimensions of spiritual direction, along with our trust in God, which moves us forward by grace and knowledge in pursuit of the mystery of perfection. Jesus said, "I am the Way, the Truth, and the Life" (the preparation, partnership and purpose) and when He said this He was giving us three progressive steps of a lifetime pursuit moving us forward into the mystery of perfection. It is the Word, Walk and Wise Witness and was there from the beginning.

Christianity is based on an image: Jesus the Christ. Jesus, the very image of God, invites us to participate fully in a pursuit into a mysterious Way (step one is "Follow Me" – Move Forward) that leads us into a richer and deeper experience of Truth in partnership with Him (step two- Pursue the Mystery of Perfection by Growing in Grace and in Knowledge) and from which one can then build the only true life for a believer, a life fully redeemed and lived in sincere connection to Christ ((step three- Living the Christ-life – and "Feed My Sheep") in which the circuits are completed that connect with God, others and creation as we feed on His Word and share it with all those who thirst and hunger for His righteousness.

This move forward into the mystery of perfection is no small undertaking. The Apostle Paul described the pain involved in the process: "Oh my dear children! I feel as if I'm going through labor pains for you again, and they will continue until Christ is fully developed in your lives." (Galatians 4:19 NLV) Moving forward in pursuit of the mystery of perfection gives birth to new dimensions of precious possibilities in God as we labor tirelessly to grow in grace and knowledge of Jesus Christ, our Lord and Savior, guided by the spiritual direction of the Holy Spirit to fulfill God's perfect plan according to the will of God the Father.

The mystery of perfection occurs when God, in His grace, invades- through knowledge of His Word, Way and Wise Witness - the destructiveness of suffering that resulted from the fall of man and uses the pain and the witness of the hurts, wounds and inconsistencies for His redemptive purposes in us. The hurts were hammered, the wounds were nailed into place and the inconsistencies of our being cut off from the root of God's plan like a piece of wood become a cross that only God Himself could bare. Thus, the wounded are welcome by His death, burial and resurrection to pursue the fullness of an intimate and personal relationship with Christ and through the Word, Walk and Wise Witness as we prepare, partner and participate in His suffering and redemptive purposes as His priesthood.

We are often unexpectedly thrust into this pursuit of the mystery of perfection by failure, loss, injury, illness, pain, abandonment, exploitation, and unfulfilled desires shaking our foundations and exposing our deepest longings and weaknesses. Because suffering affects us profoundly, it can also be a deeply transformative encounter with our vulnerability, giving us the opportunity to grow in grace and knowledge of God, ourselves, and deepening our experience of personal intimacy with the community of grace, and the body of Christ thus growing in Christ likeness.

In the crucible of these experiences of suffering in life, our souls revealed in affliction, moves us forward as we learn to commit ourselves more deeply to the redemptive purposes of God. As a result, we grow in our clarity, capacity, commitment, and consciousness to exercise faith, hope, and love in the midst of our troubles, tragedies, temptations and trials. The community of grace uses our adversity to move us forward into the mystery of perfection to shape our souls – and spread the purpose, possibilities and power of grace through the Word, Walk and Wise Witness of our pursuit.

So the mystery of perfection includes the fellowship of His sufferings. "I want to know Christ and the power of His resurrection and the fellowship of sharing in his sufferings, becoming like him in his death, and so, somehow, to attain to the resurrection from the dead" (Philippians 3:10-11). The fellowship of suffering joins us with those who share little else in common. The intimate knowledge of our own pain allows us to enter into the suffering of others as a community of faith and awakens us to the pain of God and the suffering of Christ through the community of grace.

THE CHURCH: *The Fellowship of His Suffering*

When we identify more fully with Christ's struggle and sacrifice through the growth in grace and knowledge of our own pain our gratitude for his sacrifice and his grace deepens. Just as Jesus' death was a necessary step before his resurrection, so our death to ourselves in suffering allows us to experience more of the power, promise, and purpose of His resurrection and the comfort of His incarnational embrace according to Philippians 3:10.

When we become a sincere Christian and part of the community of faith, it is not the end according to Apostle Paul, but the beginning. Our experiences of the pursuit of the mystery of perfection, so transforms our lives that growth happens through the grace and knowledge of Christ, the power is received in partnership with His suffering, his purpose in death, and his power in the promise of His resurrection and the realization of His love through the intimacy of His incarnational embrace. The bible agrees where it says, "Yes, and everyone who wants to live a godly life in Christ Jesus will suffer persecution." (2 Timothy 3:12)

It was a personal experience ("I want to know Christ") as Paul walked with Christ, prayed, obeyed His word, His will and His way, and sought to glorify His name as a wise witness that moved Paul forward into the mystery of perfection. When he was living under law, all Paul had was a set of rules to pursue. But now he had a friend, a Master, a constant Companion personally with him as he pursued the mystery of perfection to live a fully redeemed life in Christ.

In Scripture, vision is the ability to see, according to God's choosing, what God has done in the heavens so that it may be accomplished on earth. This is the heaven and earth project. Life knocks us down again and again; in the suffering it's easy to lose hope. But it is often not the flashiest or most gifted people who succeed. It is often the humble, dependable people who tenaciously pursue Christ-like perfection and even in the pain refuse to give up or give in thus encountering through faith by grace and knowledge the heaven and earth project and the mystery of perfection.

The apostle Paul was that kind of person. He pursued the mystery of perfection. In 2 Corinthians 4:16-18, he wrote: "Therefore we do not lose heart. Though outwardly we are wasting away, yet inwardly we are being renewed day by day; For our light and momentary troubles are achieving for us an eternal glory that far outweighs them all. So we fix our eyes not on what is seen, but on what is unseen. For what is seen is temporary, but what is unseen is eternal." (2 Corinthians 1:5; I Peter 4:1; 2 Timothy 3:12)

The Apostle Paul's outlook allowed him to undergo intense hardship and pain with an unwavering faith in God and a continued passionate pursuit of the mysteries of God's glory in Christ. For Paul, it wasn't as much a matter of will and determination as it was a matter of vision and perspective. It is painfully obvious that our bodies in this life wear out, our time on this planet is brief, and none of us knows how many days we have left. We ought to be thankful every day we find ourselves on top of the ground and the ground is not on top of us. However long our stay here is, compared to eternity, it's not even a blip on the screen. But our inner man is actually growing stronger as our outer man is growing weaker. That's how it's supposed to be. We ought to "grow in grace and in knowledge of our Lord and Savior Jesus Christ to Him be Glory both now and forever" (2 Peter 3:18).

Our hardships on this earth are temporary; the glory we will inherit is eternal. Our troubles are light; eternal glory is weighty. In Romans 8:18 Paul says, "I consider that our present sufferings are not worth comparing with the glory that will be revealed in us." That is not a perspective we will find reinforced in our world, our homes or even sadly in our churches today. That perspective is not found in the world; it is found only in the Word. Rather than reading and receiving life from The Los Angeles or New York Times, we ought to be reading the possibilities in the promises found in God's Word. By basing our outlook on what we find in the Bible, we can suffer in hope because we know that God's glorious future for us will somehow reach back, redemptively, into the pain of our past and cause even it to work for our ultimate benefit. Our goal in life as sincere believers who make up the community of faith should be to live a fully redeemed life in Christ in the fellowship of His suffering. What then can we render unto God for all of His many benefits?

The Practical Manifestation of Perfection

Jesus does not ask us to give up living, but to accept newness and a fullness of life that only He can give. The conversion and convergence of your strengths, passion, and genesis capacity (in other words what we were created for) when fully engaged becomes life in its fullest or living the fully redeemed life in Christ called Christ-life.

The human being has a deep-rooted tendency to "think only of self", to regard one's own person as the center of interest and to see oneself as the standard against which to gauge everything. One who chooses to follow Christ, on the other hand, avoids being wrapped up in himself and does not evaluate things according to self interest. He looks on life in terms of gift and gratitude, not in terms of conquest and possession. Life in its fullness is only lived in self-giving, and that is the fruit of the grace of Christ: an existence that is free and in communion with God and neighbor.

It is the obligation of all who believe in Christ to provide this vision that is divinely directed though it may be a mystery to both those leading and to those being led. The vision from heaven to the Sincere Church was given as instruction to grow in grace and in knowledge of the Lord Jesus Christ (2 Peter 3:18); this growth toward maturity calls for His Sincere Church, it's visionary leaders and those who follow and believe to become a committed body of believers who are filled with love that comes from a pure heart, a clear conscience, and sincere faith (I Timothy 1:5).

As a Sincerely Empowered Church where the wounded are welcome, the faithful have fellowship and the voiceless are empowered to speak their destiny, this vision calls for us to be examples for all believers in what we say, in the way we live, in the way we love ourselves and one another, in our faith and in how we reflect a life that is lived fully redeemed in fellowship with Christ. We are also according to (I Timothy 4:11) instructed to teach these things and insist that everyone learn them. This is why we work hard and continue to struggle together because our hope is in the living God, who is the Savior Christ Jesus of all people and particularly of all sincere believers pursuing the mystery of perfection by growing in grace and knowledge.

The key to this vision is our commitment to synergistically surrendering our hearts, sharing our lives, and being shaped through the study of the Word, and realized through our faithful service to the plan of Almighty God so that everyone will see our progress (I Timothy 4:15-16). As we pursue the mysteries of Godly perfection and bring forth the active embrace and empowered purpose of God into our lives we fully live out the Christ-life in grace and knowledge.

As a faithful living temple of Christ, we are commanded to grow spiritually so that the whole world can see our spiritual progress and seek to imitate it by pursuing this mystery of perfection. Christians have made the gospel about so many things … things other than Christ. When Jesus Christ is the focus then this convergence in Him brings everything together and gives them significance, reality, and meaning which moves us into the mystery of independent development of similar characteristics which can be seen as similarity of habits or creating an environment or atmosphere that causes us to passionately seek Him over all else.

Without him, all things lose their value. Without him as our focus, all things are but detached pieces of truth floating around. When the community of grace is distorted in its sincere reflection as His sincere church, like shattered pieces of a fallen star we look for a twinkle instead of the fullness of true light, life and the genuine leading of the Holy Spirit.

It is possible to emphasize a spiritual truth, value, virtue, or gift, yet miss Christ . . . who is the embodiment and incarnation of all spiritual truth, values, virtues, and gifts. Seek a truth, a value, a virtue, or a spiritual gift, without God and you have obtained something dead. Seek the community of grace through faith in Christ, embrace Christ, know Christ more intimately and purposefully, and you have touched him who is fully redeemed Life. And in him resides all Truth, Values, Virtues and Gifts in living color. Beauty has its meaning in the beauty of Christ, in whom is found all that makes us lovely and love. Who we love represents how we must love and He is the image expressed through the sincere church as we love with a pure heart, good conscience and sincere faith (I Tim. 1:5).

The world is constantly trying to get us to settle for less than the beauty of His holiness and the mystery of His perfect love and will for our redeemed lives. The world would have us authenticate our existence through achievements and accomplishments rather than through serving Him, and His perfect image as the sincere church He loves. Such ambition leads us into a narcissistic pragmatism where the ends justify the means. We begin to use people and treasure things. Build buildings and not people. This is how the world tells us we can find our place in this world. In stark contrast, the Word suggests that God alone can ultimately authenticate our existence.

When we pursue the mystery of perfection we do what we do with excellence for him and let him take care of the issues of significance and satisfaction, since he alone is the source of contentment for the sincere church. Christian doctrine of the bible is the system of divine instruction or teaching which seeks to make practical the meaning or mystery of the Bible in the light of human experiences such as love, significance and calling. The ministers of the gospel or this Good News are the primary channels through which the doctrines of God are to be distributed to the sincere church. They are the first ones given the commission to preach and to teach and serve the purposes of the kingdom and the people of God.

The believer is the subject to be instructed. Preaching is designed primarily for sinners, while teaching is primarily for believers. One of the mysteries being neglected is the teaching and divine instruction as we give way to bombastic stereotypical preaching to believers only, while Christ admonished preachers to teach them after they have been preached to, come into the mystery of perfection through belief, be baptized and begin moving forward in growth in the faith. Each church ought to be taught what is needed for them to grow in grace and knowledge.

What is Christianity anyway? It is Christ, Nothing more, nothing less! Christianity is not an ideology. Christianity is not a philosophy. Sincere Christianity is the "good news" that beauty, truth and goodness are found in your relationship with a person. The sincere biblical community is founded and found on the connection to that person. Conversion is more than a change in direction; it's a change in connection. This connection causes a "convergence" which is when God gives you a role to achieve in the mystery of perfection that capitalizes on your gifts and talent, your signature strengths making you alive and capable of living a fully redeemed life with clarity and capacity committed consciously as guided by the still small voice of the Holy Spirit as He leads you to grow in grace and in knowledge according to the mystery of why we were created.

The core gifts and talents God has given you to accomplish the role that He has for you in destiny are your signature strengths, your genesis capacity. These core signature strengths when fully engaged move you to experience the pursuit of the mysteries of God's perfection.

Jesus' called for "repentance" thus implying that we not view God from a distance but should move forward into the mystery of perfection and enter into a personal relationship where God is command central of the human connection and His character overflows revealing the mystery of His whole purpose for our lives. Integrity has everything to do with wholes . . . the whole person, the whole of creation, the whole of culture, the whole of the church, the community of faith, the whole truth . . . the Word.

Vision is simply the ability to see the whole. Like Apostle Paul, when the whole mystery is revealed and made manifest in Christ, we too must move forward in passionate pursuit always playing the whole tape of this revelation with our fully redeemed lives. In all of our getting we must first get an understanding growing in grace and in knowledge. In order to facilitate this we offer this manifesto to pursuing Godly perfection: 'Pursuing the Mystery of Perfection; Growing in Grace and Knowledge.'

Pursuing the Mystery of Ministry: A Letter from One Being Set Apart To Serve God

Dear Pastor Jelani,

Last Sunday you asked," what do I think or believe about ministry" I can't remember exactly but, I didn't answer because I first had to ask myself does God live in me? I've been reborn into God's family because God does live in me. (1 John 3:9). God's indwelling Holy Spirit is continually ministering to my inner soul, telling me to stay in the house with Him and if I do it is pleasing to Him.

God's mannerism is part of my life, I know when I'm walking in His fellowship and anointing, Jesus said, "My sheep hear My voice, I know them, and they follow Me" (John 10:27). When God speaks to my heart I can't go against His word, and to be part of the vision at Imani requires that I hear God's voice, for we are the temple of the living God. "I will live in them and walk among them. I will be their God, and they will be my people"' (2 Corinthians 6:16). "I will place My Spirit within you and cause you to follow My statutes and carefully observe My ordinances," (Ezekiel 36:27). God speaks to me through you Pastor because your spirit is connected to His Spirit, I've sat under your prophetic leadership for almost 9years come November.

I've learned how to study God's written word for myself, I heard him speak through prophets, and I've seen his angelic beings in worship, prayer, situations and circumstances. God is dwelling in me; and He's in my heart, so what do I think about ministry, my answer is "I'm a vessel of the living God". He speaks through me, leads me and directs me to walk in obedience under your leadership and the vision set forth at Imani. Pastor your obedience to God has been proven for the past 12 years, **God said, "I will**

make known My truth to you", I know God's truth that's why I'm with you, I'm committed to Imani's theology, which I know is spirit-filled and led.

I hang out with God to see what I'm made of & through the process I've embraced the fact that God fills me with His Holy Spirit and gives me His Holy Spirit gifts. The reason for these gifts is to equip me to go out and do the work of the ministry; to build up Christ's body and the church. In order for me to be effective in ministry I must be confident, committed, powerful, and victorious, and not forget that I am the salt and the light. Salt gives flavor to everything and wherever I go I should bring that flavor with me.

I believe with my whole heart that Imani is supposed to make people thirsty for a God-ordained life. God puts a piece of Himself in each believer so that the body of Christ may be perfected, matured and equipped to stand up for what we are supposed to be; and not be beat down and beat up. If we know who we are in Christ, we know we can be led by Christ; and we won't have to go around wondering if we hear Him or not.

Pastor I had to "grow up," in every way, in Christ Jesus so that I can help others in their process of growing up in Christ. Without God's Holy Spirit actively working at Imani, through you, given to us, I would have never gotten the closeness and relationship He wants with me. God told me to change and to do things His way. It was time for me to stop fighting God and get past old grudges. In order to serve the needs of people I must be equipped to minister the word of truth, (ex.) I spoke with someone who has their mind made up about who God is, I told them I don't debate God, and God's Holy Spirit will deal with that. I know God didn't hold it against me for not getting through to this person, their rejection of God is not a failure on my part, I told them that they were rejecting God not me and that it's their decision to reject God. Before we parted I ministered to them assuring them that if they would only seek God with all their heart they will find Him. I know the Holy Spirit will cleanse them from unrighteousness and bring about a pursuing heart for a Godly relationship with him and others. He did it for me He'll do it for them.

I've been waiting a long time for God to tell me what to do, and all along you've been saying what am I waiting for? Maybe I was waiting for it to get easier, I know the call of God is on my life – but I was waiting until it didn't cost me anything? God has called Imani to do great things, and through it all, I've had to learn to walk with God and grow up into the life He planned for me. If we allow God to perfect Himself in us, we'll learn how to live for Jesus.

Love,

Elder Jeanetta Mitchell